MUSEO
DEL
PRADO

Guide

Prado Museum

Alicia Quintana

ALDEASA

The Museum

Brambila. Main façade of the Prado Museum, around 1830

ne present-day Prado Museum was built in the reign of Spain's Charles III to enhance what was originally called the Salón del Prado (Prado Salon) and later became known as the Paseo del Prado (Prado Promenade). The Prado Salon was an ambitious urban scheme covering an area stretching from Cibeles to Atocha. King Charles, nicknamed «Madrid's best mayor» and «the stonemason», hoped to endow the capital city of his kingdoms with a monumental urban area comparable to those to be found in many other European capitals at the time. The Madrid in which he was born had improved little when he returned there as King (he later became King of Naples also). Madrid was still that ugly town of La Mancha which, suddenly converted into the capital city of the Spains by royal decree and favour of Philip II, had undergone a period of rapid, chaotic and inconsistent expansion.

The urban project which he entrusted to his engineers and architects was centred on the so-called Prado de los Jerónimos (Saint Jerome's Meadow), the monastery and church of San Jerónimo el Real which lie behind the Museum. This «prado» gave its name to the Salón, later the Paseo, and some time after, to the Museum.

The richly wooded area was adorned with monumental fountains (Cybele, Apollo or the Four Seasons, Neptune...all of them on classical themes characteristic of the closing decades of the 18th century) and with imposing, remarkable buildings which the monarch commissioned his architect Juan de Villanueva to build. These buildings were to be dedicated to the pursuit of Science, the constant concern of the enlightened despots. Along the North-South axis of the walkway, Villanueva planned what is now the Museum (which was, however, originally intended to be a Museum amd Library of Natural Sciences), the Botanical Gardens, and the Observatory, already built on higher ground in the Retiro park. Everything was planned with one great unifying criterion in mind: while inert Nature would be studied in what is now the Museum, living Nature would be studied in the neighbouring Botanical Gardens (a hexagonal building was even planned to link the two). Only the latter of these two constructions was eventually used for its intended purpose. The Observatory was used as such until very recently.

The Building

Plans for the Natural History Museum were approved by King Charles III in 1785, and work began soon after. Villanueva conceived it as an elongated building, following the axis of a light, topped gallery, its length broken by three bodies of greater volume: two cubic sections at the ends of the Gallery, and a building of basilical appearance at the central point. The North cube was organised around a circular space, with beautiful Ionic columns and a semispherical, pannelled dome on the main floor, and a crypt on the lower floor; the South cube was centred around a courtyard. Both of these constructions seem to recreate, as in fact did Neo-Classicism, the architectonic arrangements of classical antiquity: the first echoes the circular temple, and the second is reminiscent of the arrangement of rooms around a courtyard which was a feature of the Roman house or «domus». As for the central section, which Villanueva intended for academic sessions and gatherings of scholars and students of Natural History, it is clearly reminiscent of the Roman Basilica, elongated and with a curved apse at one end.

Brambila. North Rotunda of the Prado Museum, around 1830

Between Charles III's reign and the bloody events of the War of Independence which blighted the reign of his grandson, Ferdinand VII, construction work ground to a complete halt. The existing buildings were used as a cavalry quarters and gunpowder store by Napoleon's armies stationed in Madrid. In addition to the damage caused by this wartime use of the building, inevitably the people of Madrid themselves subsequently removed building materials (wooden beams, blocks of stone), forced to rebuild their houses which had sustained similar damage during the long conflict.

When Ferdinand VII, the king who founded the Royal Painting Museum (this was its first name), decided to create a museum of artworks from the Spanish monarchy's collections, he did not choose the Buenavista Palace (currently General Headquarters of the Army in the Plaza de Cibeles), although Joseph I Bonaparte had planned to use it for that purpose (though only

Original structure. Original layout of the Museum, 1785

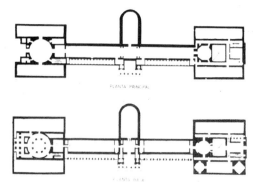

PLANTA PRINCIPAL

PLANTA BAJA

Comoroni. Litography of the North façade, around 1824

centenary. This frieze presents an allegory of
Ferdinand VII as guardian of the sciences, arts
and technology, who are shown as symbolic
figures kneeling before the royal throne; behind
the king, gods of classical mythology (Athena,
Apollo, Mercury, Neptune) appear to be
inspiring his decisions to safeguard and promote
progress.

The façade was completed with a double
decoration on the two long sections of the
Central Gallery: female allegorical sculptures in
vaulted niches, and medallions with busts of the
most prominent Spanish artists: six painters
(three on each side of the door), five sculptors
next to those on the left, and five architects
beside those on the right hand side.

The building's inadequacy for displaying its rich
reserves of art, or even for storing them in an
appropriate way, soon made the need to extend
the Museum apparent. This need was all the
greater due to modern trends in museum-
keeping which seek to provide more space for

on a sheet of paper from the Madrid Gazette),
naming it the Josephine Museum. Instead,
Ferdinand VII opted to use the building which
had been destined as a Natural History Museum
almost thirty-five years before by his enlightened
predecessor. This decision allowed building
work to recommence, and Villanueva's project
was brought to completion, using plans and a
beautiful model of considerable size (almost four
metres long); the model had been commissioned
by Villanueva himself to enable him to keep his
royal client informed about the project.

Construction was completed only ten years later,
and five years after that work began on an
iconographic decoration on the building's
exterior, which was designed by a committee set
up for this purpose. The most spectacular part of
the decoration was a grand frieze placed above
the West door, which opens onto the Paseo del
Prado and which has been known since the end
of the last century as the «Velázquez» door, after
the statue placed there to mark the painter's

Ramón Barba. Relief of the main façade, 1829-1842

the artworks on exhibit. The first extension to
the Museum was carried out in 1918, extending
the building to the rear: leaving some empty
spaces in this rear section in the form of
courtyards, on its other side a row of exhibition
rooms was added. The next enlargement took
place in the fifties, and consisted simply of
adding another row of rooms to that created a
few decades earlier. The final extension to the
building was in the sixties; the solution found
then was the only option still available, that is,
closing the courtyards to make rooms. The most
recent enlargement to the Prado has had to
involve incorporating other buildings in the
surrounding area into the Museum (Casón del
Buen Retiro, in 1971; the Villahermosa Palace
from 1985 to 1989). Further extension of the
Museum to include other nearby buildings is
planned along the same lines, since at the
moment the Prado only has exhibition space for
less than a tenth of its works of art.

e first person to have the idea of creating a
useum in Madrid, or in Spain, which amounts
 the same thing, was Anton Raffael Mengs,
inter of the Royal Chamber and Charles III's
viser in artistic matters, who suggested it to
s king; but the painter's wish never went
yond suggestion, as it was never taken up by
e monarch.

 the closing years of the same century, the
ouvre Museum was created in Revolutionary
ris in the Louvre Palace itself, using the art
easures in royal collections. This was the
spiration for the creation of many museums in
urope. The first serious official initiative to
evelop a similar Museum in Madrid was made
y Joseph I Bonaparte, in 1809, while the War of
dependence was being waged against the
ench powers. He pledged to create the
sephine Museum; however, this never went
rther than the planning stage.

he idea was taken up during the reign of
erdinand VII, who heeded requests for a
useum made by the Royal Academy of Fine
rts. He was also influenced by the special
terest shown in the project by his third wife
aría Isabel of Braganza, who has always been
ought of as the Museum's founder. The statue
f her seated figure, a Neo-Classical work by
lvarez Cubero, seems to receive visitors in the
hich has been placed in the round hall of the
elázquez entrance. Sadly, the Queen died
fore she could see the inauguration of what
as then called the Royal Painting and
culpture Museum, which took place on
9th November, 1819.

Bernardo López. Portrait of Isabel de Braganza, 1829

The first delivery of art from the royal
collections consisted of more than one thousand
five hundred works, although the Museum
opened with just over three hundred, occupying
the only available space in the North section of
the building; the other pieces had to wait until
the Museum had been completed. Subsequently,
more works from the royal collection were
incorporated over a period, including those
which were being kept in the San Fernando
Academy of Fine Arts. The collection of
paintings, sculptures and decorative arts which
gradually built up in this way continued to be

the personal property of King Ferdinand, who financed the upkeep of the Museum from his personal private funds. In these early times, the Museum only opened once a week and with severe restrictions: only those who possessed a special Court pass could visit.

When Ferdinand VII died, the Museum's pieces were to have been divided, as part of his inheritance between his two daughters: the then Queen Isabella II and her sister Luisa Fernanda. To avoid breaking up the collection, the Queen Regent María Cristina accepted the suggestion proposed by the Duke of Hijar, at that time director of the Royal Museum, that Isabella II should buy her sister's half of the collection. Thus the much-needed valuation of the pieces was begun, this being the first valuation of the Museum's assets. Soon afterwards, it was also decided to link the Royal Museum collection to the Crown rather than to the the monarch in

person, in order to avoid similar inheritance problems in the future. However, that eventuality never arose, due to the expulsion of Isabella II (1868) and the end of the Bourbon monarchy. The Museum was nationalised along with other royal assets, and became known from then on as the National Prado Museum. As well as old paintings, some of which were not from royal collections, the collection contained the works of contemporary painters who had appeared successfully in the Fine Arts Exhibitions, also instigated during the reign of Isabella II, and whose works had been bought by the State.

In 1872, the Museum was enriched by the addition of nearly three thousand works of art from the Trinity Museum, which the government of the First Republic decided to merge with the Prado. This Museum, located in the monastery which no longer exists today, had

Francisco Aznar y García. The main Hall of the Museum, published in «El Comercio» 1876

een created by one of the progressive governments of the Isabelline period with the idea of bringing together works of art from convents and monasteries in Madrid and its province, and in neighbouring provinces of central Spain, which had been dissolved following Mendizabal's Disentailment Decree).

As its art reserves went on growing, the Museum became clearly inadequate for housing this abundant artistic treasure. This gave rise to a policy of loans to official institutions and provincial museums, called «The Scattered Prado», comprising nearly four thousand pieces.

The excessively cramped exhibition of the Museum's works, and its deficient security arrangements (rendered even more problematic by the existence of living quarters for some members of staff within the Museum building itself) led to fears of a tragic fire or other disaster occurring. Furthermore, the fact that the directors, who had for some time been painters themselves (the post of Museum director was linked to that of Principal Court Painter), not only had living quarters but also workshops inside the Museum, meant that art works were coming and going all the time, which could lead to suspect activites; it also meant that dangerous inflammable materials were present in the building.

Many of those who were concerned for the safety of the Museum openly criticised this lack of security, but no measures were taken to improve the situation. In «El Liberal» newspaper, on 25th November 1891, a brilliant journalist

LA CATASTROFE
DE ANOCHE

ESPAÑA ESTA DE LUTO

INCENDIO DEL MUSEO
DE PINTURAS

Las primeras noticias

¡Noche, lóbrega noche! podríamos decir con D. Juan Nicasio Gallego, si la ocasión no fuera harto inoportuna para andarnos con floreos retóricos y si la idea de la lobreguez pudiera asociarse á la de la espantosa hoguera que en estos momentos tiene estremecido y atribulado á todo Madrid.

A las dos de la madrugada, cuando ya no nos faltaban para cerrar la presente edición más que las noticias de última hora que suelen recogerse en las oficinas del Gobierno civil, nos telefoneaban desde este centro oficial, las siguientes palabras, siniestras y aterradoras:

—El Museo del Prado está ardiendo.

Article by Mariano de Cavia published in «El Liberal». November 25st, 1891

called Mariano de Cavia daringly took the opportunity to publish false news of a fire in the Museum involving the loss of all its art reserves. This rapidly brought the matter to attention, with immediate results: director-painters were banned from having their workshops in the Museum, and twin pavillions were erected behind the main building to provide necessary accommodation for the Museum staff.

A few months before the Museum's centenary celebrations, the institution's worst ever robbery took place: in 1918 several thieves, collaborating with Museum staff, stole eleven goblets and mutilated many other pieces of the Dauphin's treasure, an important collection of precious ware amassed in the 18th century by the French Dauphin and brought to this country by his son, Philip V, the first Bourbon king. Some items were recovered still in one piece, but stripped of their precious metal decoration, while others had suffered appalling damage when the thieves removed the precious stones and cameos which adorned them.

A short while before the centenary, which was somewhat overshadowed by the theft, the Museum was reorganised by law: it was endowed with a Royal Board of Trustees, which would be responsible for steering the Museum in the right direction, and setting out its objectives. This form of administrative protection gave the Museum more flexibility and freedom, enabling it to become a leader among European and even American Museums, with a successful programme of important exhibitions. As a result, some American museums imitated the architectural organisation of the Prado.

K. Hito. Caricature published in «La Tribuna» 1918

The Civil War brought this progress to a sharp halt, as in the whole of Spain and Spanish society. From the first months of the conflict until just before it ended, Madrid became a battle front, exposing the Museum to constant danger. It was closed to the public shortly after hostilities began, and the paintings were dismounted and stowed away in the ground floor rooms, being protected from the spreading vibrations of bombings with sacks of earth. In addition, many more works of art (taken from churches and Museums in Madrid, and from El Escorial due to the intensity of the conflict in the mountains surrounding Madrid) were given refuge within its walls. This was done in the hope that the Prado could offer a protection which, objectively speaking, it could not, since it did not possess special defences or reinforcement of any kind. It was able, however, to offer a form of moral protection, based on the near certainty that neither of the sides involved

Protection of the Main Hall during the Civil War, 1936-1939

Dauphin's treasure, were taken to Valencia; from there, in response to the fluctuating situation of the war, they were later taken to Gerona; and finally to Geneva under the protection of the League of Nations. When the war ended, and with the permission of the new Spanish Government, a «Prado» exhibition was organised in Geneva, which had to be returned to Spain hurriedly and at great risk when the Second World War broke out. With much of Europe under threat and being bombarded by the Germans, the Prado's treasures had to cross French territory in night trains to escape the German planes. The paintings arrived with only slight damage to the Prado Museum, where some of the paintings which had been brought from El Escorial (for example, **The Garden of Delights** by Bosch) remained.

After the long, hard, post-war period, the new phenomenon of tourism rejuvenated the dormant Museum, causing an astonishing increase in the number of visitors.

in the conflict would be prepared to bomb the Prado Museum. Notwithstanding, it was bombed, fortunately without serious damage to the paintings.

At that point it was decided (heeding the advice of the League of Nations) to remove the most important pieces being stored in the Prado - both from its own and other collections. Three hundred and fifty-three paintings, a hundred and sixty-eight drawings, and the

Goya «The Family of Charles IV» Canvas 280 × 336 cm. (726)

The Collections in the Villanueva Building

The Prado Museum is a living, changing organism with problems of space. This means that rooms often have to be dismantled in order to house temporary exhibitions. The Museum also often lends paintings to other exhibitions for a time (frequently making it necessary to reorganise the rooms in which they were hanging). It is therefore practically impossible to produce a room-by-room itinerary, given that the contents of each room change quite often.

The visitor's programme suggested in this guide can not therefore follow a step-by-step route on the ground. It has been organised on the basis of the different schools of painting: Spanish, Flemish, Italian..., while the visitor can supplement this information with the Museum map (which also identifies its rooms by painting school) available at the entrance, which is changed every time the collections change location. For the easy identification of the pieces commented upon, the catalogue number is given along with the title, both of which are to be found on the identification plaque displayed with every painting.

Created as a Museum of Painting and Sculpture, the Museum also houses considerable collections of drawings (more than five thousand), engravings (two thousand), coins and medals (around a thousand), and almost two thousand pieces of a precious or decorative nature. As for sculpture, it is represented by more than seven hundred pieces and by a smaller quantity of sculpture fragments.

However, the enormously rich and huge painting collection (more than eight thousand six hundred paintings) has put the importance of the other collections in the shade. Even so, given the perennial problem of limited space, the Prado can only aim to exhibit the richest possible selection of its paintings (approximately one seventh) and sculptures on its two sites; the latter can only be displayed with decorative purpose in mind, as are some pieces of furniture and precious artefacts (with the exception of the exhibition of the entire Dauphin's treasure collection).

The painting collection falls into three basic groups: paintings from the royal collections (slightly more than three thousand), those which were added as a result of the merger with the Trinity Museum (slightly under two thousand), and the reserve called New Acquisitions (more than three thousand five hundred) which is the «living» section of the stocks which includes paintings ranging from the early purchases made by the Prado Museum and by the Trinity Museum while it existed, to the most recent acquisitions. These acquisitions have been made through purchases, donations and legacies, and also by public subscription.

Painting:
The Spanish Masters

The Prado houses the most impressive collection of Spanish painting in the world, especially of the «Golden Age»; it includes works ranging from the Romanesque period through to the 19th century.

Although it is rich in both quality and quantity, there are some gaps in the collection due to omissions in the Royal Collections which are its main source. The latter were amassed to suit the tastes, wishes and intentions of successive collector-monarchs, who bought or commissioned whatever pleased or interested them, and then only within the limits of their personal knowledge of art. Therefore the Castilian masters, especially the court painters of Madrid, are most fully represented in the collection. This means that there are large gaps in the representation of Art Schools of other regions —the Catalonian, Andalusian, Valencian etc.— at certain periods of their history. Another considerable shortcoming of the Royal Collections was the lack of Mediaeval Painting, though this has partly been made up for by the Trinity Museum and, especially, by fortunate new acquisitions. Because Mediaeval painting was fundamentally devotional in purpose, the early Royal collectors did not regard it as suitable for collecting, and so their acquisitions were limited to contemporary Renaissance painters. It is worthwhile pointing out that previous monarchs —such as John II of Castile and the Catholic Queen Isabella— were also great lovers and connoisseur-collectors of art, but they moved about continually (since there was no fixed Court), and this prevented them from amassing large numbers of artworks;

furthermore, when they died their possessions were often auctioned off. Some items from Isabella's predominantly Flemish collection are i fact still in existence, but none of the pieces is kept in this Museum.

As well as the uneven nature of the collection —abundance in some sections and gaps in others—, there is another characteristic aspect of the Prado's collection of Spanish painting: that is, its eminently religious and courtly tone. There are two simple explanations for the abundance of religious subject matter: first, the power that the Church has always held in this country (being painters' main and almost only client), and secondly, the inevitable religious cohesion of the Trinity Museum collection (its works being taken from convents, monasteries and temples). The courtly tone is provided by the many official portraits of the successive monarchs, their families, and the nobility.

Mediaeval painting

Despite the lack of paintings by the Spanish primitives» in the original Royal collections, over the course of time - especially in recent times - it has been possible to put together a collection which at least contains some examples of the Castilian school and, though fewer, examples of the Catalan-Aragonese and Valencian primitives. Together they afford the visitor a reasonably complete view of the historical and artistic development of Mediaeval painting.

This tour begins with two groups of Romanesque paintings which were transferred to this Museum in the nineteen forties and fifites from small Castilian churches.

The first to be added to the Museum's collections —and also the oldest, dating from the end of the 12th century— were the six fragments (transferred to canvas from the original mural) of the «**Mural paintings from the church of San Baudelio de Berlanga**» (7263 to 7268) in the province of Soria. The paintings from this chapel were exported to the United States in the twenties, and these six fragments are on indefinite loan to the Prado from the Metropolitan Museum in New York. It is surprising to find a church decoration with a secular theme (basically, hunting scenes), showing a degree of influence from moorish art and craft (ceramics, Arab ivory, miniatures of manuscripts by the Holy Man of Liébana). Romanesque painting is usually characterised by themes and techniques imported from the

Byzantine world, sometimes reworked; also, it is normally more highly coloured.

The complete group of «**Mural paintings from the Santa Cruz hermitage in Maderuelo**»★ (Segovia) (7269 to 7287) dating from the 13th century does in fact display these typical Romanesque characterisitcs: heavy outlines, brilliant colour, and great expressive force concentrated in the fixed gazes of the figures, which are represented in a non-naturalistic way,

«Santa Cruz de Maderuelo»
Detail (7269 to 7287)
Segovia

without volume or depth. The figure of Christ as the Almighty (or Pantocrat) which covers the chapel ceiling is noteworthy, as are the two central sections of the upper part and base of the building: the upper one shows the scene of Cain and Abel making their offerings to the Lamb of God, and in the lower one we see two successive moments in the Genesis story: the Creation of Adam and the First Sin. Archangels, apostles and saints decorate the margins of the side walls.

Gothic art developed in successive stages from the 14th century onwards in Spain, and the Museum can offer good examples of its most representative historical moments. The Franco-Gothic movement, also called linear Gothic due to the predominance of line and the thickness of its outlines, has been represented in the Museum since the painting «**Retable of St. Christopher**» (3150) was donated in the nineteen seventies. The flat application of colour in this piece is reminiscent of Gothic windows. The central panel of the screen (which is nevertheless in one piece, divided into «vignettes») is occupied by the saint of its title carrying the infant Christ on his shoulders, helping him to ford a river, without knowing who it is he carries. The painting shows a naive, non-naturalistic representation of the river and its fish, indicating Romanesque influence. The side panels are divided into compartments telling the story of St. Peter, St. Millan and St. Blasius. The border with castles and lions which surrounds the whole piece suggests the possibility that the altarpiece adorned a place of worship founded by royalty.

«Santa Cruz de Maderuelo»
(7269 to 7287)
Segovia

The ingenuousness of this St. Christopher contrasts with the sober seriousness of the figures in the great **«Retable of Archbishop Don Sancho de Rojas»**★ (1321), now identified as **Rodríguez de Toledo**. In this work can be detected the growing influence of the Italian art of the time, particularly the Florentine movement; this influence is responsible for the painstaking representation of volume (the bodies have «body») and the concern to convey depth and perspective (for instance, through the layout of the flagstones on the floors in some scenes). This altarpiece also has an important historical value because of the personalities represented in its central panel: the archbishop Sancho de Rojas being presented with the Mitre by the Virgin, and the Castilian prince Ferdinand, conqueror of Antequera, who became king of Aragon (the holy child is presenting him with the crown) following the Caspe Agreement.

The other large altarpiece, the so-called La Bañeza (named after its place of origin), or **«Retable of the Life of the Virgin and St. Francis»** (2545), represents a more advanced stage of Gothic art, called International-Gothic, a style which, with its tendency towards greater movement and vigour introduces a new dynamic, active tone; also new are the brilliant colour and the interest in more humble, closely observed details, which lends an anecdotal, even humorous air to the painting, and the emphasis on narrative. Of the same style are the three pieces which are still preserved from the Altarpiece **«The Legend of St. Michael»**★ (1332) by the little known **Master of Arguis** (named after the area he came from); however, in its use

of oils in some parts, and in the portrayal of clothing styles characteristic of Burgundy at that time, this work announces the arrival of the final phase of Gothic art which flourished in the last half of the 15th century: the Hispano-Flemish.

Rodríguez de Toledo
«Retable of the Archbishop Don Sancho de Rojas»
Wood panel 379 × 240 cm.
(1321)

Master of Arguis
«The Legend of St. Michael»
Wood panel 334 × 160 cm.
(1332)

The Spanish Masters:

Mediaeval painting

Fernando Gallego, who was also the first painter
to sign his works, created those works in the
collection which are most representative of the
Flemish influence; the Prado possesses a practically
unique collection of this Flanders-based school
of painting. The Flemish influence on Spanish
painting continued for a considerable time –
some of its characteristics even being preserved
well into the Italian-based Renaissance period
which followed. This influence was the cultural
and artistic result of the close relations maintained
above all by Castile, but also by Aragon, with
the northern country. There were active trading
connections, and fundamental links between the
dynasties: two children of the Catholic Monarchs
married members of the Austrian Hapsburg
family: the Archduke Philip «the Handsome»,
duke of Burgundy, married Joan «the Madwoman»),
daughter of Ferdinand and Isabella.

The works of **Fernando Gallego** reflect this
Flemish influence on Castile; and the «**Pietá or
the Fifth Sorrow**» (2998) is one of the most
representative works of this style. The influence
of Flemish painting is reflected in the spirit of
observation, the minute attention to detail, the
presence of a landscape in the background
(instead of the traditional Castilian gold), and
the typical artificiality of the fabric folds. The
dramatic style which is taken from Van der
Weyden, takes on a more tragic note here –
plainer, more austere. The Aragonese version of
the Flemish style, with its rich gold
backgrounds, is shown in «**St. Dominic
enthroned as Abbot of Silos**»★ (1323), by
Bartolomé Bermejo, an impressively
monumental work.

Bartolomé Bermejo
«St. Dominic enthroned
as Abbot of Silos»
Wood panel 242 × 130 cm.
(1323)

Pedro Berruguete's work marks the period of transition to the Renaissance in the 15th century; he blended the Hispano-Flemish tradition he assimilated in Castile with elements of the Renaissance he had learnt in Italy. Among the more than fifteen of his works preserved in the Museum, «**Auto-da-fe presided over by Saint Dominic**»★ (618) is generally regarded as the most advanced. In this panel, Berruguete affords us a reminder of the Castilian tradition in his restrained use of gold leaf, and we can detect his strong links with Flemish influences in the objective and naturalistic vision of human figures and situations. But he also incorporates a new approach, characteristic of the Renaissance: for example, we see for the first time the representation of movement (running soldiers), the study of light (the shadows projected by the soldiers, or which shape the faces of other characters), the assured control of perspective (evidenced by the various planes of depth, and further confirmed by the surprising group of figures located beneath the raised platform).

While this painting shows new techniques taken up by a Spanish painter who lived for a short time in Italy, the «**The Virgin with a Knight of Montesa**»★ (1335) by **Paolo di Sancto Leocadio** shows these innovations in the hands of an Italian artist painting in Spain, already liberated from stale techniques and concessions to Mediaeval tradition. In this respect, worthy of note are the fine study of light, the painting's sense of ideal beauty and the appearance of Renaissance architecture in the Virgin's throne. The picture is named after the donor, who is the knight of the Order of Montesa depicted smaller

in size than the other figures (as in the Gallego painting we have already seen). Another interesting fact about this painting is that it was the first to be bought for the Prado by public subscription, in 1919.

Paolo di Sancto Leocadio
«The Virgin with a Knight of Montesa
Wood panel 102 × 96 cm
(1335)

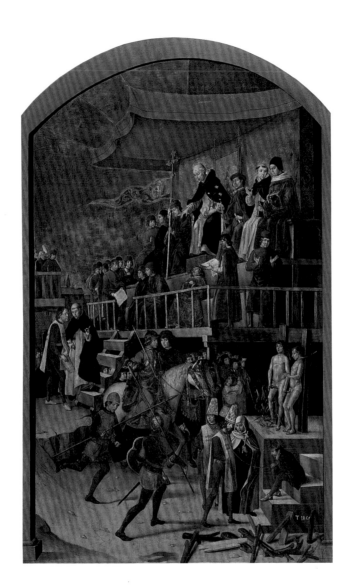

Pedro Berruguete
«Auto-da-fe presided over by St. Dominic»
Wood panel 154 × 092 cm.
(618)

Renaissance Painting

Paolo di Sancto Leocadio carried out his work in Valencia, and it was also in Valencia that the Italian Renaissance established its influence earliest and most decisively. First of all, the Spanish Renaissance participated in a Leonardesque movement which continued throughout the first third of the 16th century. The second third reflects the influence of Raphael, also tinged with Mannerism. Mannerism itself (whose main exponent was clearly El Greco), together with the new and innovative influence of Baroque brought by Italian painters who came to work in El Escorial, were the main focal points in the last third of century.

Fernando Yáñez de la Almedina, who was trained in Florence, probably in the workshop of Leonardo himself (Leonardo had a helper whom he called Ferrante Spagnuolo), is eminently Leonardesque. His monumental «**St. Catherine**»★ (2902), whose aplomb and grandeur make her like a Spanish reincarnation of the Mona Lisa, effectively signals Spain's decisive entry into the Renaissance; the softness and sweetness of her face, and the Leonardesque «sfumato» or blending technique (a special way of dealing with the problem of light by fading gradually and slowly from lighter to shadowed areas) are clear indications that Yañez is at work.

The influence of the great Raphael —including the portrayal of human figures— can be seen in the two exquisite circular paintings «**The Visitation**» (851) and «**The Martyrdom of St.**

Inés» (843), by another Valencian, **Vicente Masip**, called «the Elder» to distinguish him from his prolific son Juan Vicente Masip, known as **Juan de Juanes.** During his trip to Italy, the latter became acquainted with painting from Rome in the period after Raphael, tinged with a certain degree of Mannerism. The paintings by him which are on exhibit in the Prado are mostly pieces which together formed the high altar of the Valencian church of Saint Stephen, consisting of a cycle of works about the life of the first Christian saint. The whole collection was acquired by Charles IV; «**The Last Supper**»★ (846), is particularly outstanding, and has become one of Juanes' most well-known and popular paintings. For the first time we can observe an accomplished study in composition which has been given throrough treatment: the distribution of so many figures in a limited spac is achieved through a natural and harmonious grouping. This work also contains one of the first still lives in Spanish painting. In addition, in this series, more precisely in the episode «**The Burial of St. Stephen**» (842), we see for the first time the inclusion of the painter's self-portrait - that figure which, not participating in the scene which is unfolding before him, fixes the viewer with his gaze.

Fernando Yáñez de la Almedina
«St. Catherine»
Wood panel 212 × 112 cm.
(2902)

Juan de Juanes
«The Last Supper»
Wood panel 116 × 191 cm.
(846)

The work by **Pedro Machuca, «Descent from the Cross»**★ (3017), displays a style even more affected by Mannerism; this painting also has the added interest of being preserved in its original frame, in the form of a minutely detailed Plateresque altarpiece. This painting offers the first example of a characteristically Mannerist study of nocturnal light; also for the first time the figure of Christ is depicted in a forced position as he is being lifted from the Cross, forming a diagonal line, already showing signs of the disequilibrium in composition which was to characterise Baroque art. Despite the painting's air of Italianism (there are echoes of Leonardo, Michelangelo, Raphael, Correggio and Mannerist painters whom he met during his long period of training in Italy), a spirit of realistic observation remains, even down to humorous details such as the presence in the scene of a child with mumps, who is in lively conversation with another youngster of the same age, in front of the strange, anachronistic figure of a soldier in armour.

A similar painter on the artistic scene of this period is the Extremaduran **Luis de Morales,** nicknamed «the Divine». His style is very personal and evocative: he retains Flemish attention to detail, and evokes the style of Leonardo and of many Italian Mannerists, conserves a Venetian style of colouring and envelopes the whole in pathos and feeling which tends towards the spiritualisation and de-materialisation of human figures which El Greco would later make his own. He had to make several paintings reproducing the theme of the **«Virgin with Child»**★ (2656), whose deep

sensitivity and profound air of concentration were skilfully tuned to the religious mood of the time; the Museum itself possesses three versions

The enigmatic Morales was working when the earliest Court-based art was being produced in Madrid, which Philip II established as the capital of his kingdoms in 1561. Before that time in Spain there had been no opportunity for organised artistic activity such as this, although there had been foreign portrait painters (for instance, Titian) working for the international monarch Charles I of Spain (Charles V of Germany). The portrait painters of the Court of Philip II who produced an impressive collection of courtly figures, rigid and haughty with barely any human expression, were inspired by the Flemish school (Alonso Sánchez Coello, the most representative of these portraitists, trained with Anthonis Mor van Dashorst, called Antonio Moro in Spain), but they also incorporated Venetian elements drawn from observation of the collections belonging to Philip II and his father. Their paintings therefore bear considerable resemblance to those being produced in European courts at that time.

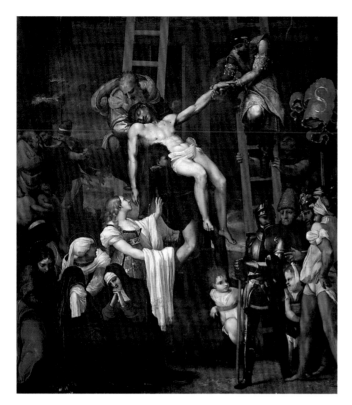

Pedro Machuca
«Descent from the Cross»
Wood panel 141 × 128 cm.
(3017)

Luis de Morales
«Virgin with Child»
Wood panel 84 × 64 cm.
(2656)

The works of **Alonso Sánchez Coello** generally
follow the same compositional scheme: the
portrait's subject depicted standing, usually
facing slightly to one side, and emerging from
dark backgrounds in which there is sometimes a
table, armchair or similar object for them to lean
on. The portrait of «**Don Carlos**» (1136), the
unfortunate son of the monarch's first marriage,
is his work, as is the portrait of his two half
sisters the «**The Infantas Isabella Clara
Eugenia and Catalina Micaela**» (1138), the
children of Philip II's third marriage with
Isabelle de Valois. He painted the Infanta
Isabella's portrait again as a young woman,
beautifully adorned and almost with a sculptured
statuesque appearance: «**Infanta Isabella Clara
Eugenia**»★ (1137), and the second Infanta, the
young duchess «**Catalina Micaela, Duchess of
Saboya**», (1139).

The name which most readily recalls the last
decades of the 16th century and even of the
beginning of the 17th, is that of **Domenicos
Theotocopolous,** or **El Greco.** Having studied
for a time in Venice and then in Rome, he
appeared on the Spanish artistic scene in 1577.
The Museum only houses one piece dating from
the period before his arrival in Spain, a small,
interesting panel, acquired in the last century,
depicting the theme of the «**Annunciation**»
(827) and carrying the clear stamp of the
Venetian school in the perspective of the
background and the colour reminiscent of
Tintoretto; and in the figures, which are
reminiscent of those of the painter Veronese.
In the first work he completed in Toledo, the
powerful «**The Trinity**»★ (824), there is a solid

Alonso Sánchez Coe
«Infanta Isabella Clara Eugen
Canvas 116 × 102 c
(11

El Greco
«The Trinity»
Canvas 300 × 179 cm.
(824)

quality, where volume is studied in a way which recalls the world of Michelangelo. These anatomically accurate figures possess a structure and strength which gives only faint hints of the Mannerism which El Greco would cultivate and take to its ultimate extremes in later works. One only need compare the body of Christ in this painting, whose body is so heavy that the Eternal Father has to make an effort to hold him up, with the almost incorporeal, de-materialised Christ in «**Resurrection**» (825), where El Greco manages to create the sensation that the figure is rising by its own strength. The guardians of his tomb, frightened and thrown down in almost unreal positions, anxiously scattering themselves throughout the limited space available, represent El Greco's finest Mannerist achievement. A similar comparison can be drawn between the small Annunciation already mentioned and the monumental «**Annunciation**» (3888) wih stylised figures, painted, as was the Resurrection work, around the turn of the century.

Portraiture was the other facet El Greco developed (he only made a few quick forays into other genres such as allegorical, mythological or landscape painting). The famous «**Nobleman with his hand on his chest**»★ (809) stands out among his foremost works. The sitter's elegant and serene melancholy lend a mysterious quality to the portrait, which has always surprised, disturbed and inspired; the sitter is the prototype of the Spanish Nobleman: «a Christian with a serious demeanour and black garments», according to the poem by Manuel Machado. A later and exceptionally beautiful work is the «**Aged Nobleman**» (806); the finer, freer

brushwork of this work testify to its later execution.

Finally, and among the many works by El Greco exhibited in his room, the visitor should note th last picture he painted, which he intended for h own burial chapel: «**The Adoration of the Shepherds**» (2788), in which he gives the painting an interior focus, a favourite Manneris technique (at a time when Mannerism had already died out in Italy and even in the neighbouring town of El Escorial, where Italian painters were concentrated). This Adoration of the Shepherds, an inward-looking composition, with its figures somewhat distorted, evokes a scene without a single reference to the physical world (neither crib, nor animals, nor gifts..), no any recognisable space.

Greco
«Nobleman with his hand on his chest»
Canvas 81 × 66 cm.
(09)

Baroque Painting

It is extremely interesting to consider Baroque art in the light of this last work by El Greco, painted in Toledo in 1614, and to compare it with one of the most interesting early Baroque works painted in the same year and same city by **Fray Juan Bautista Maino.** His **«Adoration of the Shepherds»** (3227) is a magnificent example of the new mentality of the Counter-reformation, and the new artistic sensibility of the period which El Greco chose to ignore. The latter's art —conceptual, elitist and decontextualised, only interpreted and understood by the chosen few— remained outside the new stream of religious thought which flowed from the Counter-reformation, a movement which was determined to bring the facts of religion closer to the faithful in the most accessible way. Thus, Maino's angels almost appear to be little rogues, St. Joseph is a country craftsman, the shepherds poor and weatherbeaten by their work; the offerings are marvellously realistic. The two versions could not be more different, nor could two clearer examples of artistic change be found, and yet curiously they were painted in the same year and in the same city.

Of the three overlapping phases which emerged in European Baroque art (the realist, classical, and full decorative Baroque respectively), Spanish painting lingered for a long time in the first, almost passed over the second, (which was more Italian and French) and participated in the third with large altar paintings. The two main movements seem to correspond to the two halves of the century; and in the middle, like a splendid bridge linking the two, stands the great figure of Velázquez.

The painters which had come to work at El Escorial had already brought word of the new Baroque realism and tenebrism. Maino's work has shown that these fashions were already evident in the Castilian school; other painters of this school, such as Carducho and Caxes, were also disciples of the foreign contingent at El Escorial.

Other regional schools are the Valencian and the Andalusian. **Ribalta** can be regarded as having been the first to introduce realism, in an already fully tenebrist form, to the Valencian school, which always maintained close ties with Italy, and which was therefore at the forefront when it came to introducing new techniques and ideas. In his **«Saint Francis comforted by an angel»** (1062) and his **«Christ embracing Saint Bernard»**★ (2804), we can see the two great characteristic features of early Baroque: realistic facial expressions and the naturalistic portrayal of the lamb in the former; and the use of deep shadow in the latter. This Baroque way of dealing with the problem of light —called tenebrism and also chiaroscuro— involves dramatic contrasts between areas of light and shadow, as though a powerfully focused artificial light were being directed in a certain way, as in a theatre.

Ribalta
«Christt embracing St. Bernard»
Canvas 158 × 113 cm.
(2804)

Valencia's finest champion of this Baroque style is **José de Ribera,** although he received almost all of his training in Italy (in Rome) and so settled there (in Naples) for the rest of his life. To the Caraveggesque Baroque which he learnt directly in Rome, he added a certain classical touch to his compositions, which is very characteristic of all Italian painters. His knowledge of Venetian painting also made him a splendid colourist. For this reason, Ribera's work departs slightly from the great earthy sobriety of the Spanish painters of the period. Many of his works are in Spain, since he often painted for the successive Spanish viceroys in Naples, at that time in Spain's possession. The Prado's collection is excellent. The «**St. Andrew**» (1078) is notable for its total realism in the treatment of an ageing body; «**Isaac and Jacob** (1118), for its serene composition and pictorial quality; and «**Jacob's dream**»★ (1117) for its rich, warm colours and its transparent quality in some places. The two latter works illustrate two moments in the life of the patriarch, father of the twelve tribes of Israel: first when he cheats his father into giving him the blessing due to the first-born son, and then when a stairway to heaven miraculously appears before him. «**The Martyrdom of St. Philip**»★ (previously believed to be St. Bartholomew) (1101), with the same characteristics, together with a predominance of diagonal lines in its composition, is a classic example of all that is typically Baroque.

José de Ribera
«Jacob's dream»
Canvas 179 × 233 cm.
(1117)

José de Ribera
«The Martyrdom of St. Philip»
(previously believed to be St. Bartholomew)
Canvas 234 × 234 cm.
(1101)

The great painter of the Andalusian school in the first half of the century was **Zurbarán**, who specialised in religious and monastic themes and so has become known to posterity as the «painter of friars». Compared to Ribera, Zubarán is a provincial painter, who simply juxtaposes his figures, rather than composing them: but he knew how to adapt to suit contemporary tastes and popular religious feeling. In his paintings of saints or friars (of which he painted many series for monasteries and convents in Seville) he attained a truly exceptional realism, and conveyed the qualities of objects and the textures of fabrics as no other painter could. An example of both of these are his beautiful and simple still lives, such as «**Still Life**»★ (2803), or the superbly delicate lamb in his work «**Agnus Dei**» (7293), and his episodes from the life of «**St. Peter Nolasco**»★ (1236 and 1237) or the «holy» portrait of «**St. Casilda**» (1239).

Zurbarán
«St. Peter Nolasco»
Canvas 179 × 223 cm.
(1236 and 1237)

The work of the young **Velázquez** living in Seville shared these characteristic realist and tenebrist qualities. The Prado possesses some works dating from this Sevillian period, marked by their sculpturesque appearance and earthy colours, such as the portrait of «**Sister Jerónima de la Fuente**» (2873), which has a quality of ruthless realism which no doubt the sitter found rather unwelcome, and «**The Adoration of the Magi**»★ (1166) (Reproduction on page 18) which Velázquez painted when he was only just twenty years old, yet is a mature and accomplished work. The faces of the characters represented are apparently portraits taken from the painter's own milieu: the king kneeling in the foreground may be a self-portrait, the bearded king behind him, a portrait of his father-in-law, and the Virgin and Child his wife and first daughter.

Once settled in Madrid as the king's painter resident in the Palace, Velázquez was able to become fully acquainted with his sovereign's collection of Venetian paintings; this influenced him to gradually lighten his colours, a trait which can be seen in his famous work **The Triumph of Bacchus** or «**The Topers**»★ (1170), although there is still use of chiaroscuro here, despite the fact that the scene takes place in broad daylight. He was to overhaul his style to a much greater extent, leaving chiaroscuro behind completely, after his trip to Italy paid for by the king. Another painting on a mythological theme, «**Vulcan's Forge**» (1171), is clear proof of this change, as well as being a masterly presentation of male nudes in an utterly classical style. From this canvas onwards, Velázquez advanced in the study of aerial perspective (the art of creating a

Zurbarán
«Still Life»
Canvas 46 × 84 cm.
(2803)

Velázquez
«The Triumph
of Bacchus»
or «The Topers»
Canvas 165 × 225 cm.
(1170)

three-dimensional impression by painting the air
between figures), culminating in his magnificent
achievement «**The Family of Philip IV**» or «**Las
Meninas**»★ **(The Ladies-in-waiting)** (1174).
This is the greatest work in the Prado and in
Spanish painting as a whole, and one of the most
superb artistic achievements ever created. The
artist himself appears in the composition,
painting the portrait of King Philip IV and
Queen Mariana of Austria, whose images are
reflected in the mirror in the background. The
scene is set in Velázquez's own studio, and
consists of a group of figures surrounding the
Infanta Margarita, at that moment heir to the
throne due to the death of the Infante Baltasar
Carlos. Maids and menservants surround her,
attending and accompanying her: «Las Meninas»
was the term used for those who looked after
and accompanied the royal children. The two
young ladies (Agustina Sarmiento and Isabel de
Solís), and the two dwarves (Maribarbola and
Nicolasillo) were supervised by the nun-like lady
(Marcela de Ulloa, lady-in-waiting) and the
gentleman-in-waiting, who was in charge of the
whole group. One other figure is outlined on the
steps of the staircase in the background. Apart
from the composition's beauty, his most
extraordinary achievement is the way the air is
captured —the space between the bodies of the
figures— which Velázquez was able to convey by
blurring the profiles and shading the colours of
the figures placed further away, so that they
appear to the viewer exactly how they would in
reality.

This group portrait is his portrait «par
excellence», but Velázquez painted many more of
the King (at different times of his life) and of
other members of the royal family. He represent∙
in hunting dress: **Philip IV** (1184), his brother
Cardinal-Infante Don Fernando (1186), and
his son **Infante Balthasar Carlos** (1189), and as
accomplished horseriders: **Philip III** and his
wife (1176 and 1177), **Philip IV** and his first
wife (1178 and 1179), **Baltasar Carlos** again
(1180), and also the king's close adviser and
prime minister **The Count-Duke of Olivares**
(1181).

Velázquez
«The Family of Philip IV» or «Las Meninas»
anvas 318 × 276 cm.
1174)

As Velázquez was also appointed to various palace posts, and was the King's artistic adviser, it was his job to decide on the decoration of the Salón de Reinos (Kingdoms Hall), the centrepiece of the large palacial complex in the Buen Retiro park, which had already begun when he returned from his second visit to Italy. For this decorative programme, which was to involve adorning the walls of this hall with pictures commemorating victorious battles of the reign, Velázquez reserved for himself the chance to paint «**The Surrender of Breda**»★ (1172), also called «The Lances»; this picture has always been considered a model of Spanish gallantry, since the conquerer is depicted preventing the defeated general from performing the humiliating gesture of kneeling down before him.

Apparently, the paintings of «**Jesters**» (1201, 1202, 1204, 1205, 1198, 1199, 1200) decorated another palace, in this case a hunting lodge on the Pardo Mount (an area outside Madrid) called The Parada Tower. It is always surprising and moving to note the way in which, without losing his tragic realism, Velázquez makes these characters so pleasant, portraying them as deeply human, tender, with a noble seriousness.

Velázquez's technique, which he went on developing in painting after painting (although he certainly painted little), drove him to achievements which seem almost modernist, such as the free brushstrokes, his treatment of light and handling of colour, which make him a predecessor of artistic movements such as Impressionism, far ahead of his time. For this see his two studies of light at two different moments

of the day, the two small pictures of «**The Medici Gardens in Rome**» (1210 and 1211), and the freedom of the assured, easy brushwork in the glorious «**Mercury and Argus**» (1175). And above all, see the marvellous «**The Tapestry-Weavers**»★ (1173), in which, as always, he brings to life a mythological theme, by dressing it in everyday garments, here in a tapestry workshop. The fable of a weaving contest between Arachne and her rival Athena appears in the background amid a riot of colour and light which is already fully impressionistic.

The second half of the century, marked by the development of Velázquez himself in this country, and internationally by the rise of Rubens and his influence, sees the appearance in the Madrid school of the showy, decorative Baroque style. This fully-fledged Baroque is to be found especially in large, triumphal altar pictures, full of movement. A good example of this is «**The Triumph of St. Hermengild**»★ (833) by **Herrera the Younger**, and «**The Triumph of St. Augustine**» (664) by **Claudio Coello**. And there are other examples of this dynamic, colourful style from Madrid.

In Andalusia, this uplifting and spectacular visual quality was transformed into something calmer in the hands of **Bartolomé Esteban Murillo**, whose work reflects the birth of a new sensibility inclined towards tenderer, kinder values, and a reassertion of the sense of mystery in human and familiar things. All of his charming pictures of children representing Holy characters share this quality: «**The Good Shepherd**»★ (962) or «**The Holy Children with the Shell**» (964), and especially his Immaculate Conceptions. Pictures of the Virgin with this name – a favourite theme of the Sevillians – were already in existence, but it was Murillo who forever established the characteristic features of this Marian theme. Of the four examples housed in the Prado, the following are particularly noteworthy: the «**The Immaculate Conception of El Escorial**» (972) in which Mary appears as almost an adolescent, and «**The Immaculate Conception of the Priests**» or «**of Soult**»★ (2809), in which the Virgin appears as a beautiful Andalusian woman. This work takes its

two names first from having been produced for the Priests' Hospital in Sevilla, and secondly from having been taken away by the French Marshal Soult. His heirs auctioned the work, it was bought by the Louvre, and returned to Spai in the nineteen forties as part of an agreement signed with Marshal Petain's government.

Murillo
«The Good Shepherd»
Canvas 123 × 101 cm.
(962)

Murillo
«The Immaculate Conception of the Priests» or «of Soult»
Canvas 274 × 190 cm.
(2809)

errera «The Younger»
The Triumph of St. Hermenegild»
anvas 328 × 229 cm.
333)

18th Century Painting. Goya

In the eighteenth century, Spain was ruled by a new dynasty —the French Bourbons— after the death of the last remaining king of the House of Austria (Charles II, in 1700) without an heir. During this period, the Spanish artistic scene was absorbing French and Italian influences, which were increasingly taught by the Royal Academy of Fine Arts, founded by Philip V and further shaped by his son Ferdinand VI. In its early period, this institution lay in the hands of foreign artists who had come to work on the construction of a new Royal Palace which was to substitute the Alcázar of the House of Austria which had burnt down (in 1734). Anton Raffael Mengs, Charles III's artistic adviser, steered the institution's course during the rest of that king's reign.

The Academy's training- which sought to encourage a very European approach of serene moderation to Spanish architects, sculptors and painters - produced artists who were both highly technically skilled (Anton Raffael Mengs soaring above them all) and prolific: for example, the Bayeu brothers (Goya's brothers-in-law), Mariano Salvador Maella, or Antonio Carnicero. But it would seem that all of them have been overshadowed in recent art history by the powerful artistic personality of Goya, whose work is represented in the Museum by a magnificent collection of nearly one hundred and thirty paintings and numerous drawings. The work of other interesting artists who, like Goya, kept out of the Academy mainstream also seems to pale beside his; this is the case with Paret and Meléndez.

Goya's artistic personality cannot be reduced to the conventional categories of art history: period and style. Straddling two historical periods, Goya was able, through a long process of self-development, to work as a Rococo, Neo Classical and Romantic painter; he was even a precursor of Impressionism and even of Expressionism. Goya is the grand genius of Spanish painting, prolific and multi-faceted: he painted tapestry cartoons and paintings on all kinds of themes, produced drawings and made engravings using a variety of techniques...

Of the rich collection of Goya's work brought together in the Museum (it is worth remembering that Goya was still alive when the Museum was first opened, and there were only two of his pictures in its initial collection), the large number of tapestry cartoons is remarkable - painting these was his first job at Court. The Prado possesses nearly fifty of the fifty-five he painted altogether for the Royal Tapestry Factory. The Museum usually displays a group of these together - a series of four cartoons which were produced for the King's Dining Room in the Pardo lodge. They are dedicated to Spring, «**The Flower Girls**» (793); Summer, «**The Threshing-floor**» (794); Autumn, «**The Wine Harvest**»* (795); and Winter, «**The Snowstorm**» (798). It is worthwhile pointing out the almost impressionist mastery with which Goya presents the city in the background of the cartoon Spring, with such assured and impressionistic brushstrokes as to make the master weavers' work considerably more difficult, which was apparently often the case. I

Goya
«The Wine Harvest»
Canvas 275 × 190 cm.
(795)

ne takes a closer look, one can see how Goya
aptures the whole of this city and its buildings
ith no more than a few indistinct and
nrecognisable touches. The Summer cartoon
as marvellously warm tones, dominated by
arious shades of yellow due to the presence of
e gathered sheaves. The basket of grapes in

The Wine Harvest is one of the best still-lives in
Spanish painting. And in his depiction of Winter,
Goya, who was well-informed and aware of
social problems, criticises the penury and poor
living conditions of country people, who here
appear hardly protected from the cold by their
shapeless clothing.

Of the many portraits which Goya painted
(portraiture was undoubtedly his main activity),
without doubt the most remarkable are the
individual portraits of members of the Royal
Family, produced in his capacity as Principal
Court Painter of Charles IV. Along with many
other portraits of private individuals, there are
different portraits of «**Charles III in hunting
costume**»* (737), of «**Charles IV**» (719, 727,
740), and his wife «**Queen María Luisa**» (720,
728, 2862), his brother and sister (nos. 729, 733)
and his children (730, 731). The four latter works
were preliminary sketches for the large painting
«**Charles IV and his family**»* (726)
(Reproduction on page 16), the great group
portrait in the tradition of other royal families
(Philip IV's by Velazquez and Philip V's by Van
Loo). Goya practiced - his self-portrait appears
on the canvas as did Velázquez's - exactly what
he always preached: he only acknowledged three
masters in his art: «Velázquez, Rembrandt and
nature». The painting is splendid both
technically and in its colours and study of light,
yet it is nevertheless far from evoking a tacit
respect for the royal portrait sitters such as that
which Velázquez takes pride in displaying in The
Maids of Honour. Goya's own face, and even his
way of positioning his royal sitters, give an
indication of just how far he was from
portraying the image which the monarchy -by
then obsolete and inoperative - wished to
convey, harking back to a distant age of dynastic
glory.

Among the portraits of private individuals, those
deserving particular mention are those of his
own family - ranging from the «**Self-portrait**»*

(723), to the portraits of his wife «**Josefa Bayeu
de Goya**» (722), his brother-in-law, who
introduced him to the court, «**The painter
Francisco Bayeu**» (721), and his grandson
«**Marianito Goya**»; the latter painting is usually
housed in the Prado but does not belong to it.
Among his portraits of friends, who were also
important figures in political, artistic, social and
literary circles of the time, the group portrait
«**The Duke and Duchess of Osuna with their
children**» (739) is remarkable -a pleasant family
group with a particulary true and graceful
depiction of the children.

177. T

Goya
«Carlos III»
Lienzo 208 × 126 cm.
(737)

oya
Self-portrait»
anvas 46 × 35 cm.
23)

Genre painting subjects are present in the painting collection (over and above those Goya had already done in his cartoons for tapestries) such as the graceful «**A goader on Horseback**» (744). But «**The Clothed Maja**»★ (741) and «**The Nude Maja**»★ (742), are the most well-known paintings of this type, and are the most mythical and polemical of Goya's works. They have this reputation not only because of the figure they depict but also because of whom they may have been intended for and their air of scandal and mystery. This was based on the rumour that the portrait sitter may have been the Duchess of Alba, although there is absolutely no documentary evidence to back up this suspicion. Both paintings were in minister Godoy's collection, and it is believed that together they form a kind of ribald joke, frequent at that time, whereby the clothed portrait was hung so as to cover the nude one.

A far cry from this cheerful painting of sheer enjoyment are the paintings Goya dedicated to the tragic, bloody events of the War of Independence (as well as a series of engravings entitled aptly Disasters of War). «**The Second of May, 1808, in Madrid: the Charge of the Mamelukes**»★ (748) and «**The Third of May, 1808, in Madrid: Executions on Príncipe Pío hill**»★ (749) are the two most important historical pictures in Spanish painting, and have always been regarded as emblems of the Spanish people's struggle for liberty and independence. Goya painted these two canvasses six years after the events which they commemorate took place, in 1814, when Ferdinand VII was about to return to the Spanish throne; both pictures adorned the

Goy
«The Clothed Maja
Canvas 95 × 190 cr
(74

Goy
«The Nude Maja
Canvas 97 × 190 cr
(74

Arch of Triumph which was erected for the «Awaited» king's ceremonial entry into the capital. In «**The Charge of the Mamelukes**» (the simplfied title of the first of these paintings) Goya gives concrete expression to all that characteristic violence of movement and colouring which would later define the Romanticism of Delacroix. In the second, which also carries a simplified title, «**Executions at Moncloa**», Goya created the first, embryonic example of Expressionism - a twentieth century artistic movement: its intensity and tragedy, without names or recognisable heroes, make this painting into a universal statement against war.

The dramatic and distorted features of the men being executed relate this painting to Goya's somewhat later group of «**Black Paintings**» (754-767) which he hung in the salon and dining-room of the house beside the Manzanares River, called la «Quinta de Sordo», which he bought in 1819. These are the works of an old, isolated and embittered man, surrounded by the ghosts of bad memories. The artist painted his subjects - gloomy and extreme -directly onto an unprepared wall (they must have been painted using fresco technique). After Goya's death the paintings were affected by damp due to the nearby river; they were then removed from the walls and transferred to canvas in 1873; and donated to the Prado in 1881. «**Duel with Cudgels**» (758), the «**Witches' Sabbath (Aquellare)**» (761), the disturbing «**Dog Half-submerged**» (767) and the bloody «**Saturn devouring one of his sons**»★ (763) are the best-known of these paintings.

Goya
«The Thrird of May, 1808, in Madrid:
Executions on Príncipe Pío Hill»
Canvas 266 × 345 cm.
(749)

Goya
«The Second of May, 1808, in Madrid:
the Charge of the Mamelukes»
Canvas 266 × 345 cm.
(748)

Goya
«Saturn devouring one of his sons»
anvas 146 × 83 cm.
763)

Painting:
The Italian Masters

Italian paintings constitute the third largest collection housed by the Prado, forming a nucleus of works which is the envy of many Italian Museums, not only because of the collection's size (around eight hundred works), but also because of its generally very high quality. Most of the paintings are from the Royal Collections, commissioned directly by Spanish monarchs from artists in Italy; there are also paintings by Italian artists working in Spain. Subsequent purchases and donations have made it possible to complete a splendid collection.

Modern Italian painting has is roots in the 14th century (Trecento) and the 15th century (Quattrocento); however, these early origins are the least well represented in the Collection, for historical reasons. The Castilian and Aragonese Monarchs reigning during this period of rebirth in Western art - the Catholic Monarchs themselves - were more attracted by Flemish painting, which they found more in tune with the religious inclinations of the period, and which was backed up by strong political and economic ties which had built up since Mediaeval times. Thus, there is little painting in the Museum dating from this period of Italian Art.

The oldest Italian paintings the Prado has to offer, dating from the 14th century, are the two exquisite tablets of «The Life of Saint Eloi» (2841 and 2842) recently attributed to the anonymous **Master of the Madonna of Mercy**, from Florence, and which probably formed part of the predella (lower panel or platform) of an altar. Its creator clearly belonged to the artists'

circle known as the «Giotteschi», who were thus named because their works reflect Giotto's artistic achievements in the depiction of monumental figures and the fullness of his garment folds; but he is also influenced by the Sienese School of Duccio, in the elegance of his forms and his attention to the anecdotal and everyday (such as the weighing of the gold for the King's throne which was Eloi's job as goldsmith).

In these paintings we can still see Mediaeval architectural forms, and they do not yet employ Renaissance perspective. Both of these obstacles to progress have been overcome in the piece which is the Museum's most representative picture of the first half of the 15th century (the Quattrocento): «**The Annunciation**»★ (15) by **Fra Angelico**, which was added to the Museum in the middle of the last century. The architectural background to the scene is already Renaissance here: there are classical columns and semi-circular arches (although the intersecting vaults inside the small temple are a lingering touch of the Gothic), and linear perspective has been fully achieved, with lines of perspective converging in the room which appears in the background. The profound religious spirit and devotion to be found in Fra Angelico's work (which is the reason for his nickname: his real name was Fra Giovanni da Fiesole) is fundamentally Mediaeval, yet he explored it afresh through Renaissance forms: his interest in volume and in the proportions of his human figures also testify to this. In the main area of the tablet two scenes are depicted side by side: the Annunciation and the Expulsion of Adam and

ra Angelico
The Annunciation»
ood panel 194 × 194 cm.
5)

Eve from Paradise, and on the predella or bench are various scenes from the life of the Virgin located on five small —almost miniaturist— tablets (Angelico had begun to work in the field of miniaturism); the small size does not prevent us appreciating the graceful attitudes of the figures or the sumptuousness of their garments. The five tablets depict The Birth of the Virgin, her Bretrothal, the Visitation, the Epiphany, the Presentation of the Child at the Temple, and her Death.

The first half of the 15th century, which in the Museum is represented by Fra Angelico, saw the decisive beginning of the Italian Renaissance. This was followed in the second half of the century by a period which the saw the culmination of the often experimental efforts of earlier painters. This «quattrocentist» splendour is brought to us in the Museum by prominent painters representing the various regional schools of the period.

The Florentine School is represented by three paintings by **Sandro Botticelli**, with the proverbially aristocratic air of distinction and the dignified interpretation of a theme which define him and his age so well. Botticelli relishes ideal beauty, and employs an extremely painstaking, exquisite style. These characteristics are all to be seen in the three tablets «**The story of Nastagio degli Onesti**»★ (2838, 2839, 2840). The three pieces, which no doubt were taken from a decorative wedding arch, narrate three successive episodes from one of the stories from Bocaccio's Decameron. The plot, which can be followed as in a series of vignettes by viewing the three

paintings in a row (the last scene is missing, currently in a private American collection), tells how the melancholy young Nastagio, rejected by his beloved, goes walking in lonely woods, where he has a dramatic vision: he sees a young knight condemned forever to re-enact a scene in which he hunts down his beloved and kills her - this is their eternal punishment for his suicide and her disdain. When he finds out that the scene of the hunt is repeated at certain times, he organises a country banquet at the spot, to which he invites his beloved, who obviously changes her mind and decides to marry him. Th missing tablet depicts the wedding celebrations in which they are united.

Sandro Bottice
«The Story of Nastagio degli Onesti
(2838, 2839 and 284(
3 wood panels. Each 82 × 140 cm

Only the School of Padua, in the North of Italy, attained the great heights reached by the Florentine School in the second half of the 15th century. A figure of fundamental importance was **Andrea Mantegna**, represented in this Museum by one of his masterpieces: «**The Death of the Virgin**»★ (248), one of the Prado's treasures. Despite its small size, in this painting we can see the masterly way in which Mantegna handled perspective, light and colour: all combined to create a monumentality which gives the composition an air of grandeur, in spite of its small format: the architectural forms frame the scene, the apostles are almost like classical statues, and the grief caused by the event is conveyed as being contained and quietly restrained in its austere sadness.

At the end of the 15th century the Venetian School began its ascent, showing early signs of the splendid heights it was to reach in the sixteenth. **Antonio Messina** is considered representative of the School during this period – a strange painter, with original ideas and a very advanced technique. He was born and brought up in his native Sicily and in the nearby city of Naples; he then settled in Venice after a long stay in Flanders, bringing with him Flemish characteristics such as the technique of preparing oil paints, a penetrating ability to capture everyday reality, and the spirit of observation expressed in minute details and forms. The Prado's splendid example of his work, «**Dead Christ supported by an Angel**»★ (3092), demonstrates better than most of his works precisely this combination of a Flemish training (in the taste for detail and the colouring) and an

Italian temperament, which is constantly concerned with the characters' monumentality and with facial expressions; thus, the dramatic and cadaverous face of Christ offers a counterpoint to the sweet, sorrowful features of the tearful angel. There is also a masterly contrast between the pathos of the scene and the serene lightness of the sky.

Of the great painters of the Italian 16th century (the Cinquecento), Leonardo, Michelangelo and Raphael, only the latter is represented in the Prado (although the Raphael collection is certainly very good). The absence of Leonardo i partly made up for by two interesting paintings in the Museum. One is «**The Holy Family with Saint John**» (242) by **Bernadino Luini**, one of the most important Renaissance painters in Lombardy; many aspects of this painting show signs of the great Master's training: both at a fundamental level in the modelling of the human form, and in the Virgin's delicate smile and in the peculiarly transparent quality of the chiaroscuro. It is possible that the painting is derived from a drawing of Leonardo's; it was attributed to the Master when it was part of the Royal Collections. The other work which even more closely recalls the great Italian artist, is the old copy of «**The Mona Lisa**» (504), which differs from the original in the Louvre in its lack of a landscape background (the Prado's copy has a black background) and its slightly different size. Experts disagree as to the identity of the painter; this work, though only a copy, is nevertheless very fine; it certainly brings to the Prado that mysterious aura of suggestion which has made Leonardo's work so famous.

Andrea Mantegna
«The Death of the Virgin»
Wood panel 54 × 42 cm.
(248)

Antonello de Messina
«Dead Christ supported by an Angel»
Wood panel 74 × 51 cm.
(3092)

Nothing, however, can compensate for the absence of Michelangelo, and the Prado is one of many European Museums which suffer from this gap in their collections. However, the Museum houses and extremely valuable collection of works by **Raffaelo de Urbino**, not only in size (eight works together in one place is unusual), but also because the works cover so many different facets of the Master and show the stages of his artistic development. These works were added to the Royal Collections during the 16th and 17th centuries.

The work which best represents his juvenile, Florentine stage is «**The Holy Family with a Lamb**»★ (296) in which we still detect the influence of Loenardo (basically, in the triangular composition and the use of sfumato technique, a delicate blending effect) and which shows a very careful attention to detail in the depiction of the landscape. From his period in Rome, the magnificent «**Madonna with a Fish**» (297) is on exhibit, a marvellous work of serene symmetry and orderly, monumental composition; this work on a mystical theme (the Virgin with various saints) is named after the fish brought by the young Tobias, accompanied by the Angel who instructed him to cure his father's blindness with the fish's bile.

It is often necessary to identify Raphael's «Holy Families» and «Virgins with Child» by alluding to some detail of the composition, since he used this theme repeatedly in his works. Thus, for example, «**The Holy Family under an Oak Tree**» (303) or «**Madonna with a Rose**» (302), although the rose was added at a later date.

The popularly called «**Pasmo de Sicilia**» (Spanish for «Sicilian Wonder»), its official title «**Christ falls on the way to Calvary**»★ (298), has more miraculous legend attached to it than any other work in the Prado. It was saved from the shipwrecked boat carrying it to its destination (the Sicilian church of Lo Spasimo i, Palermo; the adaptation of this name gives the painting its nickname), it left there for Spain, amid riotous protests against its sale to Philip I' of Spain; it escaped unharmed from the Alcazar fire in the 18th century; and it was kidnapped b the French during the War of Independence and taken to Paris where it was transferred from the three large panels on which Raphael had painted it onto a canvas support which has preserved th painting magnificently. The Spanish monarchs always considered it to be the most valuable piece in the collection; records show that, in the evaluation of the Museum's paintings carried ou following the death of Ferdinand VII, already mentioned in this guide, it was valued at more than thirty times more than Velázquez's Tapestry-Weavers. Its complex composition and the rich variety of pose and gesture of its numerous figures made this painting famous from the moment it was created, in 1517, at the beginning of the Cinquecento period: nothing had ever been painted before with such grand aims or such assured results.

Raffaello de Urbino
«Christ falls on the way to Calvary»
Wood panel, transferred to Canvas. 318 × 229 cm.
(298)

Raffaello de Urbino
«The Holy Family with a Lamb»
Wood panel 29 × 21 cm.
(296)

«**Portrait of a Cardinal**»★ (299) is an excellent example of Raphael's skill in portraiture, and of his ability to penetrate deeply into the mind and soul of his sitters. The identity of this Church primate is not known, but he is the archetypal Renaissance Cardinal: intelligent, aloof, astute and enigmatic. The painting is also a magnificent example of Raphael's skillful liberal application of colour, here using only one basic tone.

The Museum has works by other painters in Raphael's artistic circle; of these, **Andrea del Sarto** and his «**Mystic Subject**» (334), which is indisputably one of his masterpieces, deserve particular mention. In this painting, the play of facial expressions, ranging from amusement to melancholy, reveals Del Sarto's typical tenderness, which gives his work its originality. His work in general owes its balance to Raphael, its delicate sfumato to Leonardo, and its grandeur to Michelangelo. The original poses and colour tones anticipate Mannerism.

Another Master of great distinction, also working in Northern Italy (in Parma) could be regarded as anticipating the typical concerns of the next great artistic epoch, the Baroque. His name was Antonio Allegri, called **Correggio** after his birthplace. His «**Madonna and child with the infant Saint John**» (112) and his «**Noli me tangere**» (111) show all these advances: the display of feeling (everything is made pleasant in his works), the order of his compositions (already introducing the diagonal line in the arrangement), the symbolic use of certain colours, and the lively naturalism of his landscapes.

The Museum has a good selection of more thoroughly Mannerist painters. Mannerism is th term used to refer to a style increasingly regarded as important (and it is now acknowleged that it covered a longer period of time than previously thought). From being considered merely a means of transition from th Renaissance to the Baroque, it is now recognise as a style in its own right - a style and mode of thought and action which replaced the serene Classicism of the Renaissance at its height. Thes were times of the Lutheran Reformation, the los of popular belief in religious authority, the downfall of powerful absolute monarchies, the foundering of spiritual certainties, times of personal insecurity and restlessness. No doubt we in the twentieth century have wished to cast the last half of the 16th century in such a role —intellectual, affected, and restless— because w regard ourselves as sharing this identity. The term Mannerism comes from the Italian word «maniera» (way, method) and it was first used to refer to painters who, looking for a successful seam to mine, worked «alla maniera de» («in the manner of») —Raphael, Michelangelo— exaggerating characteristics and aspects which had raised the great Masters of the Classical Renaissance to such heights.

Raffaello de Urbino
«Portrait of a Cardinal»
Canvas 79 × 61 cm.
(299)

Common features of pictorial Mannerism are the sensual rhythms around which compositions are formed, the exquisite colouring, the elegant forms and refined interpretation of situations. El Greco's work was to become the most delirious and exasperating manifestation of this aesthetic spirit - anti-naturalist, symbolic and disturbing. However, among Italian Mannerist painters, **Parmigianino**, earlier than El Greco, is outstanding; without doubt it was he who contributed more than any other to the spiritual stylisation, undulating rhythms and almost symphonic harmonies of colour. «**The Holy Family with an Angel**» (283) is his work, marvellously aware of curved lines. Good examples of the concern about fitting figures into the limits of a composition are «**The Holy Family**» (329) by **Jacopino del Conte**, the allegory of «**Charity**» (476) by **Carlo Portelli**, and the «**Madonna with child and two Angels**» (477), by Francesco de' Rossi, called **Salviati**. The work of the painter Federigo Fiori, called **Barocci**, marks the beginning of a change towards the Baroque which would follow, to the extent that the word Baroque is thought possibly to originate from his nickname; the theatrical effects of his compositions and the artificial light which breathes life into his work «**The Nativity of Christ**»★ (18) do indeed anticipate Baroque aesthetics.

Meanwhile in Venice, the powerful Venetian School had continued to develop; the Prado has the best collection of this School in the world, especially because of the high quality of this group of works. **Giorgione**, the mysterious and enigmatic founder of this School, apparently

painted «**The Virgin and child between St. Anthony and St. Roch**» (288), which would be one of the few of his works to be preserved, due to his early death. Some scholars prefer to attribute this work to the young Titian.

The Venetian School gave full expression to the opulent and refined world of that rich trading Republic. This school made great contributions to Renaissance Art in Italy and throughout the world: for example, innovations in the use of light and colour, and in perspective and background space; also its great ability to capture that special relationship between the human being and the world that surrounds him. The great triad of Venetian painters —Titian, Tintoretto and Veronese— is magnificently represented in the Museum, due to the special fondness the Spanish royal collectors Charles V and Philip II had for the work of these artists. Subsequent monarchs continued to acquire Venetian painting until a collection was built up. This is why Spanish painters ranging from Velázquez to the great decorative painters of Madrid, observing these works in royal residences, were inspired to follow their example

arocci
The Nativity of Christ»
anvas 136 × 107 cm.
8)

The young **Titian** was responsible for the magnificent panel **«The Virgin and Child with St. George and St. Catherine»** (434), sometimes titled «St. Catherine's mystic Betrothal», a marvellous painting for the roundness and sensuality of its forms, bathed in a golden light which caresses the rich fabrics and is reflected in the shining armour. A long and valuable series of paintings (more than thirty works) cover all aspects of his work.

Among the mythological works, **«Bacchanal»**★ (418) **«The Garden of Loves»** (419), **«Venus and Adonis»**★ (422) and **«Danae receiving a Shower of Gold»** (425), are the most outstanding. The first two of these were painted to decorate the Duke of Ferrara's study. The first depicts the arrival of Dionysus, the god of wine, on the fortunate island of Naxos which was dedicated to him because its springs flowed with wine rather than water; its inhabitants are in the middle of their wine festival celebrations. The «Garden of Loves» depicts a large number of Cupids jumping, running, playing and tussling, in a variety of poses. In «Venus and Adonis» one is surprised by the movement and the original composition; in «Danae» the Venetian tendency to dissolve forms is shown to the full.

Among religious pictures, the Prado can offer the intense drama of **«Ecce Homo»** (437), which the Emperor Charles V kept with him at his retreat in Yuste, along with **«The Glory»** (432), which is of considerable historic interest since it offers us the sight of the Emperor Charles, his wife the Empress, his son Philip II and other members of the Royal Family, all wrapped in

shrouds. The various versions of the **«Mater Dolorosa»** (443 and 444), **«The Entombment of Christ»** (440), and **«Jesus and the Cyrenian»** (439) complete the religious panorama of Titian's works, and again present us with the free and unrestrained technique of his last works.

Titian
«Bacchanal»
Canvas 175 × 193 cm.
(418)

Titian
«Venus and Adonis»
Canvas 186 × 207 cm.
(422)

The Museum's Titian collection covers all
aspects of his approach as a portrait artist,
ranging from the excellent military portraits such
as «**The Marquis del Vasto addressing his
troops**» (417) to much more gentle, courtly
paintings, such as «**The Emperor Charles V**»
(409) in a calm, restful pose, and that of his wife
«**The Empress Isabella**» (415), a posthumous
portrait, using other pictures as models, which is
why the facial expression is not firmer. Although
in military dress, the portrait of «**Philip II**» (411)
has a certain courtly quality about it, having
been produced to send to the English Queen
Mary Tudor, the Spanish prince's future second
wife. The most famous portrait of the Emperor
Charles has a publicist and political tone about
it, on horseback in a pose which recalls the
heroes of the former Roman Empire: «**The
Emperor Charles V at Mühlberg**»★ (410).
Properly speaking, it is more a portrait of the
idea of empire than of an imperial ruler himself;
but the sitter's melancholy expression (he was ill
and nearing retirement) nevertheless reveals great
psychological depth.

All Titian's portraits, including the magnificent
«**Self- portrait**» (407), with its blurred,
unfinished outlines, completed in the last years
of his life, share a certain sober colouring and
make clear allusions to the Classical world; they
were to have long-lasting influence on Spanish
portraiture, from contemporary painters (for
example, Sánchez Coello) to El Greco and
Velázquez.

tian
he Emperor Charles V in Mühlberg»
nvas 332 × 279 cm.
0)

The two other great figures of the Venetian School are also very much in evidence in the Prado's exhibition rooms. Jacopo di Robusti, called **Tintoretto**, who liked to use colder colours than Titian, is at his peak in portraits such as «**The Nobleman with the Golden Chain**» (378) or «**Lady revealing her bosom**» (382). However, in his large compositions he is considerably more Mannerist than Titian. The best example of this is his grand «**Christ washing the disciples' feet**»★ (2824) bought by the Spanish king Philip IV in the auction held to sell off the assets of the executed Charles I of England. This work employs grand theatrical effects: large figures in the foreground frame the whole piece, and conduct the viewer's gaze towards the scene in the painting and on into the distant background. In order to produce this sensation, Tintoretto employs certain technical effects; for example, the lines converging in the background following the different-coloured flagstones, the play of light and shadow which create a three–dimensional effect, and even the play of glances between different figures in the painting. This creation of the sensation of real space is emphasised even further in the painting's foreground through effects which produce an impression of space underneath the tablecloth; Velázquez may well have found in this effect a source of inspiration for the aerial perspective of «Las Meninas».

By way of contrast with the large «Washing of the disciples' feet», six small canvasses by Tintoretto are on display; these have been taken from a ceiling decoration bought by Velázquez in Italy for king Philip IV. All of then (386, 388, 389, 394, 395, 396) deal with Biblical themes;

one of them is titled «**Judith and Holofernes**» (389) a subject which Tintoretto painted on other occasions (390 and 391), on a larger scale and with strong contrasts of light and shade which are almost Baroque.

Paolo Caliari, called **Veronese** after his birthplace, is undoubtedly the painter who most exactly defines the characteristics of the Venetian school, and his works in the Prado testify to this: sensitivity, a love of life, a love of landscape and an interest in colour. There are works of his on Biblical themes, from the refined and exquisite small gem «**Moses rescued from the Nile**» (502) to the severe, elegant «**Susannah and the Elders**» (483), where his persistent interest in the basis of monumental architectural forms is also very evident. Architecture figures more prominently in one of his most accomplished renderings of a New Testament subject, «**Christ with the Doctors in the Temple**»★ (491): this picture is one of the finest achievements in the creation of space in the whole of Renaissance painting.

Finally, among his other works, an exceptionally beautiful painting on a mythological subject is worth particular mention: «**Venus and Adonis**» (482), which was also bought by Velázquez; he must surely have been seduced by the atmosphere suggesting air vibration which envelops the whole scene; the group of figures is reposed and quiet: Venus watches over the sleeping Adonis, and a cupid is trying to restrain a dog which is moving about because it has just heard the horn announcing the hunt in which Adonis will later die.

ntoretto
hrist washing the disciples' feet»
nvas 210×533 cm.
324)

Veronese
«Christ with the Doctors in the Temple»
Canvas 236×430 cm.
(491)

The Museum's ability to exhibit Italian Baroque, dating from the 17th century, is usually rather limited due to problems of space; however, certain masterpieces are usually present. These are just some of the works which belong to he three main artistic movements of the period: tenebrist naturalism at the beginning of the century, pure classicism somewhat later, and then fully-fledged decorative Baroque.

Tenebrist naturalism can be seen in the painting «**David victorious over Goliath**»★ (65) by **Caravaggio** (his real name was Michelangelo Merisi), the painter who initiated the movement with his daring and innovative solutions. The composition is surprisingly harmonious considering it is compressed into such a small space, equally surprising is the expressiveness with which the subject is presented; all of this is enhanced by the powerful contrast of light and dark which gave rise to tenebrism and chiaroscuro.

Classicism, also anti-naturalist, but always with a tendency to «improve» upon Nature, correcting and perfecting it in pursuit of an ideal beauty, is always beautiful and serene, endowed with a sense of balance which results from a thorough and studied treatment. Its pioneers and its great masters were different members of the Bolognese dynasty of Carracci. The Prado possesses works by **Anibale Carracci**, the most prominent and influential painter of the group: the exceptionally beautiful «**Assumption of the Virgin**» (75), grandiose and solemn, and an opulent, Baroque «**Venus, Adonis and Cupid**» (2631). Of the nearly twenty works the Museum possesses by **Guido Reni**, another of the founding masters of

Classicism, who nevertheless also made use of Tenebrist solutions, one of his loveliest works is exhibited: «**Hippomenes and Atalanta**»★ (3090) This painting relates the confrontation between two young contenders in a race, and tells of how the astute Hippomenes throws some golden apples to the ground, thus distracting Atlanta's attention and taking her mind off the race.

The last great beacon of Italian Baroque who is represented in this Museum is **Luca Giordano**, better known in Spain, where he lived and worked for ten years, as Lucas Jordán. Furthermore, his work epitomises the decorative Baroque movement. He was born and trained in Naples (he was influenced by Ribera) and Rome (dominated at that time by the great fresco artists and decorators of temple ceilings); he was also acquainted with the Florentine heritage and the Venetian collections. Added to all this, he was gifted with a prolific creative facility and worked with prodigious speed; this ability earned him the nickname «Fa presto» (Do it quickly) which, as legend has it, was the phrase his father used to urge him on in his early days as a painter. In Spain he left decorativist traces on ceilings in El Escorial and the Buen Retiro palace (the one covering the ceiling of the Salon in the Casón is his) and also in some temples. More than seventy of his works are kept in the Museum, but only a few are normally on show, for reasons of space. In any event, the royal portraits on horseback of «**Charles II**», the last monarch of the House of Austria for whom he worked (197 and 2762), and that of his second wife «**Queen Mariana of Neuburg**» (198 and 2763) are particulary noteworthy.

Caravaggio
«David victorious over Goliath»
Canvas 110 × 91 cm.
(65)

Guido Reni
«Hippomenes and
Atalanta»
Canvas 206 × 297 cm.
(3090)

Italian 18th century painting is rarely exhibited, for the reasons of space already noted. Of the works in the Museum from various Italian Schools we will only consider the interesting conributions made by the Napolitan painter **Corrado Giaquinto** and the Venetian Tiepolo. Many of the former's sketches for temple and Palace frescoes are preserved (especially for various rooms in the Royal Palace in Madrid), along with some splendid easel pictures, full of elegant sensuality, such as the very beautiful allegory «**Justice and Peace**»★ (104). The Venetian School is undoubtedly the one which best displays the aesthetic apotheosis of the eighteenth century (still steeped in the assumptions of the Baroque decorative period). The most famous and cosmopolitan figure was **Giambattista Tiepolo**, who created decorative frescoes employing wide and grandiose illusionist perspectives, which made him famous throughout Europe. He arrived at Court in

Madrid when he was already old (nearly seventy), accompanied by his sons Domenico and Lorenzo, carrying out various composition for the Royal Palace (such as that which adorns the Throne Room). During the eight years in which he lived in Spain (where he died) he also did paintings for the Convent Church of San Pascual in Aranjuez, now in the Prado's hands. These beautiful paintings suffered from the passion for Neo-Classicism nourished by another great painter (who had a different ideology and aesthetic) also called to the Spanis Court by Charles III: Mengs. He arranged for them to be taken down, and during this operation, they were either carelessly of intentionally damaged, and substituted by som of his own. Five of these paintings of Tiepolo some cases only fragments) are usually on display in the Prado: we single out the extraordinary «**The Immaculate Conception**» (363) and «**Angel bearing the Eucharist**» (36

Corrado Giaquinto
«**Justice and Peace**»
Canvas 216 × 325 cm.
(104)

Giambattista Tiepolo
«The Immaculate Conception»
Canvas 279 × 152 cm.
(363)

Painting:
The Flemish Masters

The Flemish painting collection occupies a well–deserved place of honour in the Prado Museum; it is second only to the Spanish collection and is certainly of the same stature as the Italian. It encompasses works ranging from the 15th century painters, called the Primitives, up to the 17th century when this School (which should really be called the Low Countries School) split into two distinct artistic movements, when the two territories which previously made up the Spanish Low Countries were divided. Painting from what has henceforth been known as Belgium keeps the name Flemish; the term Dutch is reserved for painting from the United Provinces (which at that point became independent from the Spanish Empire they had together belonged to, so forming the country of Holland).

The Flemish painting collection (the Dutch will be dealt with in a later chapter) is exceptional both for the large number and high quality of its works. The exhibition of these treasures is always restricted in terms of numbers, due to the Museum's problems of limited space: for example, not even all of Rubens' works can be displayed. It is regarded as an excellent collection, not only because it allows the visitor to follow the artistic development of the School, but also because of the large number of «major works» it contains. Most of the works were acquired by monarchs and prominent members of the Spanish nobility at the time they were painted; for this reason, they are fully documented and surrounded by an almost charismatic aura of authenticity.

There had been much interest in Burgundy-Flemish art since the Middle Ages. The economic ties between Burgundy and Castile (based on the wool trade) were consolidated by political links forged by Ferdinand the Catholic Monarch. These bonds were sealed by dynastic relationships: Juan and Juana, the children of the Catholic Monarchs, married Margarita and Felipe, Austrian archduchess and archduke, the latter also Duke of Burgundy. It is therefore no coincidence that successive monarchs were interested in acquiring Flemish works or in hiring the services of Flemish painters; Michel Zitow and Jan van Flanders worked in Castile for Isabella the Catholic Queen herself.

The Flemish collection as a whole encompasses three centuries, and three clear stages of evolution. The first of these corresponds to the 15th century, the works of the so-called «Flemish primitives», still steeped in Mediaevalism (if we compare them with the sparkling innovators of the Italian Renaissance) but nevertheless responsible for introducing new ideas and fresh solutions - different from the Italian aesthetic and the principles of perspective which define the Renaissance, but perhaps equally valuable.

A varied group of outstanding painters emerge during the course of the 15th century. The tour begins with School's founders, the brothers Jan and Hübert van Eyck; however, of their circle, the Prado now only possesses a few copies and interpretations attributed to followers (although there were important works by Jan van Eyck in the Royal Collections). This is the case with

The Fountain of Grace» (1511), undoubtedly
by one of the Master's close followers, and
perhaps a copy of an original by him; there are
good grounds for relating it, due to its technique
and theme, with famous works by Van Eyck,
such as the polyptych in St. Bavon cathedral in
Ghent, which has a similar scenographic
structure. The fountain from which eucharistic
forms well up separates two floor areas, which
hold groups representing the Vanquished
Synagogue and the Triumphant Church
respectively; we then pass from angelic
musicians and singers to the celestial figures of
the Lamb, Christ, the Virgin and St. John.

The tour of the «Primitives» begins with the so-
called Master of Flemalle, now generally
considered to have been **Robert Campin**, a
somewhat mysterious artist, and still difficult to
identify; especially since occasionally his works
are easily attributed to the young Van der
Weyden, one of his followers. Particularly
outstanding are the two side-panels of a triptych
(of which the central panel has been lost) which
figure «**St. John the Baptist and the
Franciscan Heinrich von Werl**» (1513)
appearing against a background where fine
details are used to create the concept of space.
Space is used in a similar way to recreate the
house of «**St. Barbara**»★ (1514). Both interiors
are marvellously, minutely detailed: household
objects, furniture and objets d'art are depicted
with the same studied and painstaking care as
the human figures. Both works are unsurpassable
in the realistic depiction of flowing, rumpled
draperies - another characteristic of this School.
In both cases there are views looking onto a

Robert Campin
«St. Barbara»
Canvas 101 × 47 cm.
(1514)

landscape, executed with an exquisite handling of colour and light, and worked with the same minute attention to detail as the subjects in the foreground. (See, for instance, the tower which in the second of these paintings identifies the woman depicted as St. Barabara).

The application of oil paints, reintroduced by the Van Eyck brothers when they invented an oily drying ingredient, gives Flemish primitive painting that special glowing, almost enamelled quality, further emphasised by the vivid colours, often applied in very thin coats onto a prepared white ground. These and the other characteristics mentioned can be observed at all stages of the developing artistic movement which links Capin to **Roger Van der Weyden.**

Gothic archaisms disappear in the work of the masterly Weyden; in his pursuit of the presentation of the human side of religious events he achieved greater dramatic intensity and expressive skill. He is a master of composition and his figures are elegant; furthermore, he was tremendously inventive. The Museum is proud to be able to present one of his most perfect and dramatic works: «**Deposition**»★ (2825). Here the deliberate absence of background concentrates the attention on the scene unfolding before our eyes. The two figures at either end appear to enclose the scene in brackets; the group, which could have been monotonous given the number of figures and the small space available, is a clever counterpoint of forms and spaces, broken by the movement brought into play by the rhythms created by the parallel postures of Christ and the Virgin. The expression of tragic

emotion on the faces of the figures, and the detailed depiction of their garments —one can even sense the tactile qualities of draperies and objects— make this Deposition one of the Museum's masterpieces. It arrived in the Museum via the Royal Collections, inherited by Philip II from his aunt Maria of Hungary; the monarch had even had a copy of it made previously, by Michel van Coxcie, which is now kept in El Escorial Monastery. The original must have been part of a triptych (the two side panels have been lost); the whole work was painted for the Brotherhood of Crossbowmen in Louvain. Also by Van der Weyden, the «**Pietà**» (2540), is exhibited showing similarly dramatic faces and poses. The figure of the donor, equal in size to the other figures in the scene, and participating in it, confirms the fact that attention to fine detail and the spirit of observation made the Flemish painters especially gifted as portrait painters.

Roger Van der Weyden
«Deposition»
Wood panel 220 × 262 cm.
(2825)

Hans Memling is definitely thought to have trained in Weyden's workshop, and greatly popularised the forms and compositions originated by his Master. He was more painstaking and preoccupied with fine detail than the latter, but his work is less dramatic, and therefore less gripping. His figures appear in calmer poses, his compositions are more serene. This is the case with his large, sweet and harmonious triptych «**The Nativity. The Adoration of the Kings. The Purification**» (1557), a finely detailed and delicate piece. Although very advanced as regards the landscape in the background, which toys with linear perspective, the artist's attempts to deal with the problem of light are still clumsy; for example, in the first panel, St. Joseph is shown carrying a candle which does not appear to illuminate anything, so failing to give the impression that the scene is at night.

Gerard David occupies a period of transition to the 16th century; he has a very individual style, and is able to endow his religious figures with a special, almost intimate softness. See, for example, the exquisite Virgin and Child in his «**Rest on the Flight into Egypt**» (2643), in which we can see his geat interest in landscape which also plays an important part in this scene. Landscape assumed still greater importance in the painting of **Joachim Patinir**, another artist whose work spans two centuries. In his painting also called «**Rest on the Flight into Egypt**» (1611), the landscape plays the most important role, and furthermore contains multiple additional scenes. Some of these are deliciously anecdotal, such as St. Joseph with the pale of

milk (on the left), the pedestals of Egyptian statues which according to legend tumbled dow. as the divine child passed by (on the right), or even the country harvest scene which also has a traditional explanation: the sheaves are supposed to have grown extremely quickly in order to hide the child from his pursuers. Patenier's love of landscape led him occasionally to collaborate with other painters, in which he only did the background, and another artist was responsible for the main scene; for example, the magnificent panel «**The Temptation of St. Anthony**»★ (1615), was painted in collaboration with **Quentin Massys**. Here Patenier's wide panorama of sober grandeur is superimposed with the contrastingly beautiful and repugnant figures with which Massys wished to surround the Saint. The latter, from Antwerp, was also on of the first to introduce innovations of the Italia. Renaissance into the Low Countries; in his work one can detect the influence of Leonardo and Raphael, although he never actually broke with long Flemish tradition; this can be seen in his work «**Christ presented to the people**» (2801).

oachim Patinir
«The Temptation of St. Anthony»
Wood panel 155 × 173 cm.
1615)

The most original and most representative figure of this turn-of-the-century period (somewhat ealier than Patenier and Massys), is **Hieronymous van Aeken Bosch**. He took his nickname from the last syllable of the name of his birthplace: Hertogenbosch. The name was altered to «**El Bosco**» in Spain, where there were a large number of his works, which is an indication of the interest generated by his work here. Philip II was especially interested, and gave orders to buy any Bosch painting that was for sale, and the Prado's magnificent group of Bosch paintings (including some of his most major works) comes from the Royal Collection. In these paintings one is always struck by Bosch's astonishing imaginative capacity to conceive of scenes and themes and to develop an entire moral critique of contemporary society. He has been described in all kinds of ways - as mocking, enigmatic, critical, heretical..., even in his own 16th century; many of his works were destroyed, censured as disrespectful and heretical.

Although there is little known about his life, he is thought to have been a cultured man, acquainted with the religious and secular literature of his time (for which he acts as a kind of illustrator), but he must also have been an ordinary, down-to-earth man, who knew the popular sayings and proverbs which he often comments on in his paintings. One thing which we do know for certain about him is that he was linked to the so-called Brethren of the Common Life which, as well as being a religious organisation very aware of contemporary issues and very critical of society, organised processions and theatrical tableaux. From this

Mediaeval theatre- and carnival-world Bosch gleaned many themes which are still surprising today. It is almost possible to speak of Bosch as the first Surrealist painter; and also the first Expressionist, since he sacrifices the potential beauty of his figures to the expressiveness of the theme as a whole.

There are examples on display which cover the long period of development of his special approach. The earliest of his works is «**The Cure for Folly**»* (2056), which may be a criticism of fraudulent Mediaeval quacks and of the idea that madness was caused by a stone forming in the head, although some have preferred to see in it a reference to a castration ceremony. Another work of his early years is the curious work «**The Table of the Seven Deadly Sins**» (2822): the central circle encloses a figure of the raised Christ which looks like the pupil of a large eye formed by concentric circles; in the circle surrounding Christ are the words «cave, cave, dominus videt» (be careful, be careful, God sees us). The largest circle holds seven scenes of different sizes, each of which contains a commentary on one of the deadly sins, bearing its Latin name. The four smaller circles placed in the corners of the painting refer to the so-called Four Last Things: judgment, death, hell and heaven.

The theme of hell —one of Bosch's great specialities— is much more fully explored in the right-hand panels of his two most famous triptychs. The first of these is called «**The Hay Cart**» (2052), which depicts on its left-hand panel different moments in the Creation of

Adam and Eve, their temptaion and sin, and the Expulsion from Paradise. The central panel is dominated by the hay cart which gives the work its name; this is an allusion to a Flemish proverb which runs «the world is a hay cart from which every one takes what he can». Noblemen and earthly potentates follow the cart in stately calvacade, constantly within easy reach of its pleasures; the poor people, however, gather round trying to grab what they can, ready to kill to get what they want. The clergy, represented by the nuns in the bottom right of the painting, contrive a scheme to bring sacks of pleasure right into the convent. The gesture of God, in the upper part of the panel, seems almost one of impotence in the face of the human madness unfolding before Him on the earth. The right-hand panel depicts hell, which is where this mad pursuit of pleasure will inevitably lead: the final punishment.

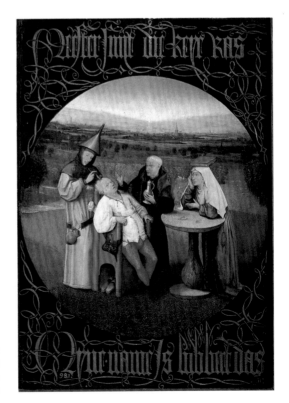

Bosch
«The Cure for Folly»
Wood panel 48 × 35 cm.
(2056)

In «**The Garden of Delights**»★ (2823), Bosch reaches his most spectacular heights. This is Bosch's best-known and most often studied work; it is also the one which has been subject to the most varied interpretation. Again, the Creation and Hell frame a world of earthly pleasures. This time the pleaures are represented symbolically by red fruits (strawberries, madroña berries...) which everyone is eagerly picking and enjoying; moreover, «no sooner has the fragrance of the fruit been smelled, than it fades away», in the words of Father Sigüenza commenting on the picture when he arrived at El Escorial at the end of the 16th century. The painting's symbolism is clear. But some have preferred to accept the interpretation which identifies the scene with the thinking of a heretical sect of the period: the so-called Brethren of the Free Spirit (or Adamites, after Adam), who supported the idea of a return to primitive purity based on complete sexual liberty and nudism (hence the connection with Adam). If this is the correct version, the strange procession around the lake in the central part of the panel would be the cortège of an inititiation ceremony performed by this sect. In contrast to the general nudity of the scene, only one figure appears dressed, in the bottom right-hand corner of the picture, covered with an animal skin: this has been interpreted by some as St. John the Baptist (who would therefore be pointing at Eve, as the cause of all this lascivious activity) and by others as a self-portrait of Bosch. Some others interpret the large white head which stands out in the middle of the panel depicting a fantasy hell as the artist's self-portrait.

«**The Adoration of the Magi**»★ (2048), the title of another triptych by Bosch, is the scene represented in its central panel. The side panels show the painting's donators, accompanied by their respective guardian Saints, St. Peter and St. Inés. The whole piece is surrounded by an air of unreality, since there are many enigmatic aspects of the work which do not fit with the religious subject, and which are difficult to interpret; the most noticeable of these is the anomalous presence in the central scene of a strange, white, semi-naked figure, appearing through the doorway, dressed in truly opulent garments: he has been interpreted by some as the Anti-Christ.

This is one of Bosch's later paintings; «**The Temptation of Saint Anthony**» (2049) is considered to be his last work, a subject which undoubtedly gave free reign to his imagination, and which he often repeated.

Bosch
«The Garden of Delights»
Triptych on Wood 220 × 195 cm.
(2823)

Bosch
«The Adoration of the Magi»
Side panels 138 × 34. Central panel 138 × 72 cm.
(2048)

The Flemish 16th century is always a little forgotten, which in fact is the case with this period in all the Schools left in the shade beside the splendour of the Italian Renaissance. But there are Flemish figures in the 16th century who may not be unworthy of comparison with the three great Italian «prodigies» of the period. Many painters clearly show the powerful influence of Italian painting; some very Italianised artists emerged, while others preferred to stick more closely to the old Flemish techniques. In the first group, apart from Massys and his early experiments within the Flemish tradition, there are some artists who were definitely Renaissance innovators. Thus, Massys' style influenced by Leonardo gives way to a style influenced by Raphael, but more differentiated from him. This latter style is represented by Gossaert and Orley. **Jan Gossaert**, also called **Mabuse**, takes on board Italian-style grandiose and monumental tendencies, sometimes to the extent of being overdone and excessively architectural; a good example of this would be his «**The Virgin and Child**» (1930); this has opulent forms and portrays the musculature of the child in a way which recalls Michelangelo's child nudes. **Bernaerdt van Orley**'s work is finer and more delicate, and usually shows more attachment for the old Flemish techniques: for example in his «**Holy Family**» (2692), he has no objection to placing a decidedly Raphaelesque Virgin and Child alongside a St. Joseph who clearly shows Germanic influence (in the style of Dürer), and an angel bringing an offering, whose minute detail and delicately outlined figure have a characteristically Flemish air.

But the great figures of the 16th century, whose work reveals the upsurge of the old energies of the Flemish School, are Brueghel and Mor. **Pieter Bruegel «the Elder»**, the first in a long line of painters in his family, would never seek portray man as the god-like centre of the Universe conceived by the Italians; the role he gave to mankind was one of a creature dominated by Nature, bearing his burden of troubles. Thus, in his most famous work, «**The Triumph of Death**»★ (1393), he exalts nature to the point where anonymous man appears, cowering, before the terrifying drama of death: an army of skeletons is advancing, cornering humanity, and pushing it towards the grave. The work's evident social criticism —all the social classes facing death at once, and their diverse reactions (struggle, flight, impotence) to it— evokes Bosch in his finer moments. It is certain a painting of extremes, crammed with details of horror, despair, and desolation.

Anthonis Mor was the most famous portraitist of his age. He was able to distance himself from the idealising Italian concept of portraiture, and was the true pioneer of the portrait as psychological study. This was based on a choice of an indistinct background in order not to distract the observer's attention, and the sitter's expression, perceptibly revealing the person's inner depths, even appearing to return the observer's gaze. One of his masterpieces is the portrait of «**Queen Mary of England (Mary Tudor), second wife of Philip II**»★ (2108), an extraordinary image of coldness and austere elegance; it is the portrait of the woman who would later be known as «Bloody Mary» becaus

...her cruel repression of Protestantism, and ...ho was the second wife (and also the aunt) of ...e Spanish King Philip II. As well as the many ...atures of Mor's portraits which anticipate the ...er portraits of Velázquez, we are reminded of ...e later Spainsh Master in the choice of subject **«Pejerón, Jester of the Count of Benavente ...d the Duke of Alba»** (2107), perhaps the first ...inting in history of a jester (Court jesters in ...ain were also called «men of pleasure».)

Anthonis Mor
**«Queen Mary of England
(Mary Tudor)»**
Wood panel 109 × 84 cm.
(2108)

Pieter Brueghel **«The Elder».**
«The Triumph of Death»
Wood panel 117 × 162 cm.
(1393)

The great 17th century is dominated by the powerful figure of Rubens, who restores the Flemish School to its former place, at the height of Baroque painting. This School was very important and active in this century, in which a mastery of Italian techniques, with a plethora of forms and heroic figures, is added to the traditional realism and the gorgeous brilliance of colour which the Flemish school had always been renowned for. Rubens and other Flemish painters of the period fulfilled the political requirements of the by then decadent Spanish monarchy (under which what is now Belgium would remain), and served the religious ideals of the Counter-Reformation led from Rome, to which Belgium would continue to adhere. (Holland, constituted from the independent northern United Provinces, was Calvinist). The work of **Peter Paul Rubens** served these twin purposes as no other artist's work could: ranging from Arches of Triumph for ceremonial receptions of Spanish governors, to splendid religious exaltations such as the Eucharistic cartoons made for tapestries in the Descalzas Reales monastery.

There is something of everything in Rubens' work. Moreover, his astonishing personal vitality, which comes across clearly in the work, enabled him to pursue many other activities. He had a powerful personality and a potent creative imagination; he was unequalled in his impulsive, bold expression of the visual language of Baroque. This was a language of exuberant compositions, infused with dynamic energy, sumptuous richness of colour, and tumultuous rhythms underlain by an inner harmony: all

working together to produce a powerful sense c vitality. The white and swollen flesh of his female figures seems to palpitate with life, and the strength of his male heroic figures is reveale in their muscles, rippling beneath the skin.

The Prado's Rubens collection contains nearly a hundred pieces. This guide can therefore only point out a few of particular interest. Of these, one of the earliest is the splendid «**St. George**»* (1644), with its violent structural movement based on diagonal lines. Another early work, although enlarged and repainted by the artist himself nearly twenty years later, is the enormous «**Adoration of the Magi**» (1638); thi is also composed around a grand diagonal whic is projected from the figure of the infant Christ It is a spectacular, sumptuous work, harmoniou despite the piling of one figure on top of another, thanks to the carefully balanced arrangement. In the strip added later on the right-hand side of the painting (another runs across the top), Rubens has included his self-portrait, in the form of a knight dressed in purple who, though standing with his back to us, turns his head towards the observer.

ter Paul Rubens
t. George»
nvas 304 × 256 cm.
44)

Rubens painted many mythological subjects. His representation of «**The Three Graces**»★ (1670) is particularly outstanding. The palpitating flesh, the opulence and splendid vitality of the work are absolutely characteristic. Rubens kept the painting for himself (Philip IV of Spain bought it when the artist's assets were auctioned off after his death), apparently because two of these benign spirits of Nature are portraits of his wives. His second wife, who married Rubens when she was sixteen and he a widower of fifty-three, would be the permanent model for all his later works. For instance, she appears as Aphrodite (in central position, surrounded by other nudes) in «**The Judgment of Paris**» (1669), which is the most evocative of all Rubens' renderings of this Greek myth. It tells the story of how the young Paris had to decide who was the most beautiful of three goddesses, to whom he would present a golden apple (brought to him by Hermes, Zeus' messenger). The candidates are depicted with symbols associated with their deity: Athena, goddess of War, has a shield at her feet; Aphrodite, the goddess of love, is accompanied by a cupid; and Hera, Zeus' wife and goddess of the hearth, is accompanied by her symbol, the peacock. The prize offered to the surprised Paris by the winning goddess (seen here receiving the winner's garland of flowers), was the love of the most beautiful woman in the world. Since this woman is Helen, already married to the King of Sparta, Paris kidnaps her and starts the Trojan War, in which legend and history merge.

Among Rubens' portraits, particularly remarkable is the direct, simple frankness of

«**Marie de Medici**» (1685) and the dynamic, expressive power of the portrait on horseback o «**The Duke of Lerma**» (3137). In this portrait Rubens breaks with Renaissance tradition in equestrian portraits which placed horse and rid in profile, picturing the horse coming towards the observer, as though it were trying to leave the painting.

Rubens was also responsible for a considerable part of the decorative programme for the hunting palace near Madrid called Torre de la Parada, on the Pardo Mount. This small palace was decorated with hunting themes (for examp Velázquez's hunting monarchs) and mythologic subjects, inspired by Ovid's Metamorphosis, painted by Rubens. He did the sketches illustrating each of these stories, and other arti (such as Jordaens) and followers in his worksho executed the large pictures, although Rubens di keep some to do himself. Almost the complete set of these paintings is exhibited in the Museum; some of Rubens' preparatory sketche are also on display.

er Paul Rubens
e Three Graces»
od panel 221 × 181 cm.
70)

The whole of Rubens' work offers a sharp contrast to the characteristic delicacy and refinement, bordering on the rococo, of **Anton van Dyck**, although the latter in his early period while working in Rubens' workshop, was as dramatic and expressive as his Master. His personality, his work in the English Court, and the several years he spent in Italy are all important factors in his development towards a more exquisite and refined style. Van Dyck has mainly gone down in history as a fine portrait artist, who lends a particularly attractive elegance to his sitters, achieved with a mixture of half-dignified and half-flattering poses. As early as the 18th century, the essayist on Spanish art Antonio Palomina recommended the imitation of Velázquez's «realistic portraits», and of Van Dyck's «flattering» ones. Among the Van Dyck treasures housed in the Prado, the portrait of «**Maria Ruthven**» (1495), his wife, is particularly outstanding, as is the meticulous double portrait of «**Sir Endymion Porter and Van Dyck**»★ (1489); in the latter, the artist paints his own portrait next to that of his British patron, politician, collector and connoisseur of art.

The great Flemish triad of the 17th century is completed by **Jacob Jordaens**, whose work has a more popular tone and suited more down-to-earth tastes; his forms are more careless and he often disregards beauty, even running the risk of indulging a taste for vulgarity. He undoubtedly distanced himself from heroic presentations and religious triumphalism: he was more attached to the living world around him, and more interested in the immediate, real and visible. The most well-known work of his works in the Prado's collection is his «**Family Portrait**» (1549), depicting himself, his wife and daughter and a servant in the family home. But his most original work, for the immediacy of its technique which gives it an astonishingly modern air, is «**Three travelling musicians**» (1550) with bold brush-strokes and skilful use light.

Another artist whose work has spontaneity and who pays close attention to everyday life — including even the life of the most deprived members of society— is **David Teniers**, whose work anticipates the achievements of the style which would be known in the 19th century as «social» painting. It depicts popular Flemish customs, as in «**Peasants merry-making**» (1785), or «**The King drinks**» (1797), and many standard genre painting subjects, such as «**Smokers and Drinkers**» (1794). He is also the creator of a fine, famous picture, of «**The Archduke Leopold William in his picture gallery**»★ (1813), a clear example of the genre of the period which portrayed the picture galleries of collectors, the supreme example of the painting within a painting.

A long series of «minor» painters (thus called because they concentrate on genre painting) follow in the train of these major artists. Landscapes, still lives, pictures of animals, floral paintings, pictures of collectors' studies...make up the production of the rest of the 17th century, which is as far as the Prado's Flemish collection extends.

Anton van Dyck
«Sir Endymion Porter and Van Dyck»
Canavas 115 × 141 cm. oval
(1489)

David Teniers
«The Archduke Leopold William
in his picture gallery»
Copper. 106 × 129 cm.
(1813)

The French Painting

The French painting collection is next to the Spanish, Italian and Flemish collections in importance, although it falls some way behind them. It includes over three hundred pieces, mostly dating from the 17th and 18th centuries The 17th century was plagued by armed conflicts between France and Spain, though this did not prevent links being forged between ruling families. Philip IV and Charles II both had French wives, and Louis XIII and Louis XIV married Spanish infantas; this led to exchanges of portraits and gifts of artworks between the families. Other works by French artists entered the Spanish royal collections by being bought in Italy directly from painters working there. In the 18th century there were frequent artistic contacts between the two nations since both were ruled by the same Bourbon dynasty, and many French painters came to work at the Spanish court.

The collection has works by several of the most important French painters of the 17th century. The allegorical work «**Time overcome by Youth and Beauty**» (2987) must be regarded as **Simon Vouet's** masterpiece; in its use of colour and its dynamic energy, it still shows signs of his Italian training. Another painter who also spent a good part of his life in Italy, but whose work is much more tranquil, is **Nicolas Poussin**, who most clearly epitomises French Classicism, as manifest in the Classical Baroque movement. His works seems measured and balanced, and reveal a carefully intellectualised aesthetic. The Prado holds an important group of his masterpieces. «**The Triumph of David**» (2311) is a noteworthy

work on a religious theme; its treatment is so Classical that the figure who is crowning the young David seems more like the figure of Victory than an angel; all of the figures, down t the delightful, playful children, have a certain a of solemnity about them. «**Parnassus**»★ (2313) gives a cooler impression; it is a superbly ordered and harmonious composition, with an even and flowing distribution of masses, depicting a scene in which Apollo, surrounded by Muses, presides over the coronation of a poe while many other *literati* look on. The lovely nude in the centre of the canvas is an allegorica representation of Castalia, the spring which wells up on Mount Parnassus. Two landscape works by Poussin, «**Landscape with Saint Jerome**» (2304) and «**Landscape with Buildings**» (2310) introduce us to the serenely beautiful work of the other great French 17th-century artist, **Lorrain «Claudio de Lorena»** (actually called Claude Gellée). Lorrain created his own style of highly idealised landscape, always set in Classical Antiquity, and including the sea and sun and their various effects. He painted all the phases of daylight from dawn to nightfall, creating a peaceful, pastoral vision of the countryside; and, with his very personal use of colour gradations, was able to convey a sensation of unlimited depth. The human figure in his paintings merely complement the scene, and in some cases almost disappear altogether. The Prado's Lorrain collection would be difficu to equal: it includes ten exceptionally fine paintings. The best known are «**Landscape wit the finding of Moses**» (2253), and the «**Landscape with the Embarkation of St. Paula Romana at Ostia**»★ (2254): both of thes

Nicolas Poussin
«Parnassus»
Canvas 145 × 197 cm.
(1813)

paintings were part of a commission given to Lorrain during the decoration of the Buen Retiro Palace. These two pictures show him at his best in the study of light and atmosphere; for this reason they were later to inspire many artists interested in the phenomenon of light, from Corot to the Impressionists.

The Museum has recently acquired a magnificent work by **Georges de La Tour**, also from the 17th century. Hitherto, this painter's absence from the Prado's collection was always regarded as a great lack. The new acquisition is «**The Blind man playing the hurdy-gurdy**» (7613), undoubtedly one of the greatest achievements of a small output by this painter, who normally concentrated on genre subjects.

The end of the 17th centry and beginning of the 18th witnessed the development of an important School of portrait painters centred around the court of the Sun King (Louis XIV). One of the painters who undoubtedly made a major contribution to the shaping of the so-called «court» portrait —grandiloquent, pompous and consciously spectacular— was **Hyacinthe Rigaud**. Particularly remarkable are the portraits of the ostentatious, distant «**Louis XIV**»★ (2343), and of the first Bourbon King, «**Philip V**» (2337). The latter is portrayed in «Spanish style», dressed more severely, conveyed as a man with very definite political intentions. There are delightful portraits of children of this Hispano-French dynasty by other French painters: for instance «**Maria Anna Victoria of Bourbon**» (2277) on the Spanish side, by **Nicolas Largilliere**, and the charming «**Louis XV as a**

child» (2262) dressed in a long outfit like a girl by **Pierre Gobert.** Gobert was also responsible for the «mythological» portrait (in Spain at that time, portraits were done in «the divine style») «**The Duchess of Burgundy and her children**» (2274): this work includes, among others, the portraits of the future Louis XIV (the boy carrying the torch).

rrain
andscape with the Embarkation
St. Paula Romana at Ostia»
nvas 211 × 145 cm.
254)

Hyacinthe Rigaud
«Louis XIV»
Canvas 238 × 149 cm.
(2343)

The 18th century —the quintessentially French age of Rococo— is represented in the Museum by two small gems by **Antoine Watteau**, undisputed pioneer of Rococo painting. He has been defined as a painter of gallant gatherings, which is borne out by the pictures: small, intimate and elegant paintings set in dream-like places, vibrating with a lyrical melancholy, and bridging the imperceptible dividing line between painting and poetry. The two paintings by him here are «**The Marriage Contract**» (2353) and «**Gathering in a Park**» (2354). The most remarkable thing about both is the way in which the artist captures the airy, luminous atmosphere of the natural scene, endowing it with a nostalgic, dream-like quality.

Among the many French painters who settled in Spain after the Bourbons acceded to the Spanish throne, the portrait painters are undoubtedly the most important. Many of the portraits were pictures of the princes and infantas which the new Spanish royal family must have wished to send to the main branch of the family in France. **Jean Ranc** painted many of these child portraits: «**Louis I**» (2370), «**Ferdinand VI as a child**» (2333), **Charles III as a child**» (2334), sons of Philip V; and also the sketch (2376) for a larger group portrait, now lost. **Louis-Michel Van Loo**'s large and splendid portrait of the same family **The Family of Philip V**»★ (2283) was completed, however; it is a veritable dynastic gathering presented in a highly elaborate way: the family are pictured in a grand palatial salon, which opens onto a leafy garden, and listening to a concert.

Louis-Michel Van Loo
The Family of Philip V»
Canvas 406 × 511 cm.
(2283)

The Dutch Painting

The United Provinces of the Low Countries became independent from Spain when the Westphalia Peace Treaty was signed in 1648. However, this merely set the official seal on essential differences between the Northern and Southern areas of the Low Countries, although they had formed a single nation under the rule of the House of Austria since the beginning of the 16th century. These differences had existed for a long time, especially since the beginning of the Protestant Reformation.

Some painters born on Dutch soil have been included in the section on the Flemish School (such as Anthonis Mor, or Bosch himself), since it is not until the beginning of the 17th century when distinct trends can be identified. The Dutch aesthetic began to take a characteristic shape, inspired by a severe and moralising Calvinist spirit; artists worked for burghers, not for the Church or for rulers, hence the frequently small format and almost total absence of the heroic subject matter common to other Baroque styles.

In the first half of the 17th century Spain and Holland were at war; in the second half, they maintained tense diplomatic relations. The natural hostility and different tastes of the two nations meant that there was little artistic or cultural exchange between them. As a result, the Museum houses only a small Dutch collection; it only began to obtain Dutch works from the time of Philip V, the first Bourbon, in the 18th century. This collection, which despite the king's interest never grew very large, was also the most widely dispersed during the years of the French invasion and the War of Independence, since the French marshals and King Joseph I shared a certain liking for these works, small in size with a pleasant range of subjects. The Prado is therefore only able to exhibit what remains of the original collection.

The most important work and centrepiece of the collection is «**Artemisia**»★ (2132) by **Rembrandt** (Harmenszoon Van Rijn Rembrandt). It is signed and dated and fully documented. It belonged to the collection of the learned Marquis de la Ensenada, and was then bought by Charles III when the Marquis died. It is undoubtedly one of Rembrandt's masterpieces It is a simple composition, in which the solemnity and grandeur of the main character are particularly striking. Like the rest of the composition, she is enveloped by Rembrandt's characteristic evocative atmosphere, which the artist skilfully creates through the contrast between the golden light which bathes the foreground and the semi-darkness of the background. There is some doubt about the painting's subject: although it is increasingly accepted that the woman is Artemisia, Mausulus' widow, preparing to drink her husband's ashes, some commentators incline to the view that it could be Sophonisba, the wife of Masinisa, about to drink the poison sent by her husband to avoid her falling into the hands of the Roman enemy.

The «**Self-portrait**» (2808),bought by the Museum in 1939 with profits generated by the

eneva Exhibition (mentioned at the beginning
f this guidebook), is nowadays thought to be a
opy made in Rembrandt's time, but not by him.

f the hundred or so works whick go together
o form the Museum's Dutch collection, the
ajority are genre paintings by artists known as
minor» (as was the case in Flanders) because of
eir choice of subject matter —still lives,
ndscapes, paintings of animals, tavern scenes...

Rembrandt
«Artemisia»
Canvas 142 × 153 cm.
(2132)

The German Painting

The austere and sometimes tragic expressionist aesthetic generated by the German spirit was not likely, of course, to suit the tastes of the Spanish royal collectors, who were more attracted to Mediterranean sensibilities and Flemish traditions of piety. This seems to be the only explanation as to why only a small number of German works were brought into the royal collections, despite the close political and dynastic ties between Spain and the German Empire. However, it is true that the few pieces are very fine indeed, especially four paintings by Dürer, the most unique figure in the German School of the 16th century; they are accompanied by works by other first class painters of the same period. However, there is practically nothing in the Museum dating from the 17th century. The 18th century collection is enhanced by the presence in Spain of the painter Mengs, from Bohemia, hired by Charles III.

Albrecht Dürer is the foremost Renaissance painter of Nordic Europe. After a period spent in Venice, he was able to combine Italian innovations, such as the concept of ideal beauty, grandeur and the study of perspective, with the long traditions of German Gothic; he owes his realistic observation and the precise details of his compositions to the germanic spirit. The Prado is proud to possess one of the three **«Self-portraits»**★ (2179) by the artist. This one was painted when he was twenty-six years old. He appears elegantly dressed, as though he were a gentleman of noble birth: only Italian artists portrayed themselves with a similar demeanour.

Furthermore, his very low-cut garment gives him a certain Italian air which contrasts with his pale, Nordic face. On the right of the painting, under the window, appear the date (1498), and a text in German which reads «I painted my own likeness. I was twenty-six years old. Albrecht Dürer», and the characteristic anagram as a signature: A.D.

Dürer was also a scholar and wrote essays on the proportions of the human body. Perhaps his works of genius **«Adam»**★ (2177) and **«Eve»** (2178), a marvellous pair of paintings which were a gift from Philip IV to Queen Christina of Sweden, were an attempt by Dürer to put his knowledge and opinions into practice. The fourth work by Dürer in the Prado is **«Portrait of an unknown man»** (2180), one of his best male portraits, an image of seriousness and concentration which conveys a certain contained energy, no doubt a result of the small space available on the canvas.

Albrecht Dürer
«Self-portrait»
Wood panel 52 × 41 cm.
(2179)

Albrecht Dürer
«Adam»
Wood panel 209 × 81 cm.
(2177)

Hans Baldung Grien was one of Dürer's followers and friends, an odd painter whose work shows an early touch of Mannerism. Philip II owned two of his pieces, which strike the viewer with their symbolic content and a certain refinement of cruelty, lending a permanent air of strangeness, even brutality, to the works, called «**Harmony or the Three Graces**» (2219) and «**The Ages of Man and Death**» (2220).

Lucas Cranach, a contemporary of both, preferred to remain outside the influence of the Italian Renaissance, and so is the most Germanic and least refined of the three. He was a fabulous portrait painter (he painted his friend Luther). He also worked in the landscape genre, of which the Prado has two examples. They depict two separate moments during the «**Hunt in honour of Charles V near the Castle of Torgau**» (2175 and 2176). They provide an almost documentary record of an historical event: the celebrations organised by the Elector of Saxony in the Emperor's honour, at a Castle in Hartenfels.

German painting from the 18th century is confined to **Anton Raphael Mengs**'s exquisite portraits of the members of Charles III's family. These have the delicacy of porcelain and touches of the Neo-Classicism which was emerging at that time. In Spain, he painted ceilings in the Royal Palace, altar pieces and portraits, and directed the Royal Tapestry Factory and the programmes of the San Fernando Academy of Fine Arts. «**The Adoration of the Shepherds**» (2204) is one of his notable works on a religious theme; its human forms clearly owe much to Raphael, and its light effects are drawn from

Correggio; his many years in Italy explain this return to the Renaissance which did so much to foster the birth of Neo-Classicism. He painted the official portrait of **Charles III**»★ (2200), and the posthumous portrait of «**Queen Maria Amalia**» (2201), and of not less than thirteen other members of the royal family. The Museum also preserves his individual «**Self-portrait**» (2197), as well as that which appears on the left in the aforementioned «Adoration of the Shepherds»

Anton Raphael Mengs
«Charles III»
Canvas 154 × 110 cm.
(2200)

The British Painting

British painting is not well represented in the
Prado. When the Museum was founded there
was not a single painting of this School in the
royal collections. From the 16th to the 19th
centuries, Anglo-Spanish relations were
continually hostile, and somewhat unfavourable
to cultural and artistic exchange. For this reason,
the Museum's British collection is recent, having
accumulated over the course of this century,
through donations, legacies and purchases. In
any case, the collection is small, although some
fine pieces and important names figure.
Unfortunately, there is not much variety, since
the majority of the pieces are portraits, dating
from a fairly short period: the second half of the
18th century, and the first few years of the 19th.

The Prado has two fine portraits by **Joshua
Reynolds**, one of the most interesting and
important painters of the 18th century (he was
First Painter to the King and founder of the
Royal Academy), although they are not very
typical of the so-called «grand style» which he
developed for the many aristocratic portraits he
painted in a long and successful career. They are
«**Portrait of a clergyman**» (2858) and «**Portrait
of Mr. James Bourdieu**» (2986). **Thomas
Gainsborough** painted delightful portraits of
women and children, lending them an exquisite
air of elegance and aristocratic aloofness, but this
Museum only has examples of his portraits of
men; nevertheless, the portrait of his doctor
«**Isaac Henrique Seqeira**» (2979) is splendid.
There are also some works by **George Romney**,
but the best-represented artist is **Thomas**

Lawrence; we can admire the indolent gesture
of «**John Vane, Tenth Earl of Westmorland**»
(3001), or the direct, almost instantaneous
expressiveness of «**Miss Marthe Carr**»★ (3012),
both magnificent examples of his ability to
capture the personality of his sitters.

omas Lawrence
iss Marthe Carr»

nvas 76 × 64 cm.

012)

Sculpture

The Prado Museum's important and undoubtedly valuable Collection of Sculpture has always been overshadowed by the wealth of the Museum's picture collections. Nevertheless, it is not by any means an insignificant collection, being quite large (more than seven hundred pieces) and containing some very fine pieces. Unfortunately, for reasons of limited space, only a few can be exhibited, and these are displayed more as individual pieces for decorative purposes than in an ordered and meaningful group. At the time this guide was being written, a project was underway to bring the sculptures together into a few rooms dedicated exclusively to sculpture. It should be remembered that the Museum was founded as the Royal Museum of Painting and Sculpture.

The Royal Sculpture Collection, formed from the time of Philip II, did not come intact to the Museum. Many of its pieces were sent by the monarchs of the Enlightenement to the then recently created Fine Arts Academy, and any others are still decorating the Palaces and Royal Country Houses. Some of the ancient Classical sculptures which did come to the Prado were subsequently transferred to the National Archaeological Museum when it was created. And the religious sculptures taken from altars and processional floats which the Prado received from the Trinity Museum were taken to Valladolid in 1933, when the Sculpture Museum of that Castillian city was promoted to National level.

The collection includes pieces ranging from ancient statues (Sumarian, Egyptian, Ancient and Classical Greek and Roman) to 19th-century works which are exhibited in the 19th century section of the Casón del Buen Retiro.

The sculptures can be divided into four groups: Philip II's collection (made up of gifts sent from Italy, and of pieces which came from archaelogical excavations in Spain), acquisitions made by Velázquez in Italy for his sovereign Philip IV (most of them cast from moulds, due to the dificulty of obtaining original works), Philip V's purchase of the collection which had belonged to Queen Christina of Sweden (undoubtedly the best of the Prado's collections and the donation accepted by Charles IV from the scholar and collector José Nicolas de Azara, who had been Ambassador in Rome. In addition to all this, the collection was progressively enriched by commissions and portraits requested by successive monarchs from their Court Sculptors; and also by purchases made by the Museum, as a Museum, in the course of the 19th century (for example, prize-winning sculptures from the Fine Arts Exhibitions) and the 20th.

«San Ildefonso Grou
Marble 160 × 106 × 56 c
(E 2

The Classical Sculpture collection includes many series of Roman busts, part of groups which were put together representing the Twelve Caesars. But there are also more original and remarkable pieces, such as the so-called «**Venus of Madrid**» (E 44) and «**Venus with a shell**» (E 86), which used to belong to Philip II, and the «**Athena Parthenos**» (E 47), a Roman small-scale copy of the colossal sculpture of Athena which graced the Greek Parthenon. The work «**Apotheosis of Claudius**» (E 225) which was given to Philip V, is very unusual in concept and technique, and is thought to date (as does the Athena) from the second century A.D. It consists of Roman weapons and the prows of ships, in the form of a military trophy, supporting a powerful eagle with outspread wings. The bust which tops the whole piece is a copy, and must have been placed there at a later date.

The most important Classical pieces which remain to be discussed come from Queen Christina of Sweden's collection, which was one of the best Roman collections of its time (it will be remembered that the Queen abdicated, converted to Catholicism, and settled and died in Rome). The handsome group of young nudes known as the «**San Ildefonso Group**»★ (E 28) after the place in which they were found, is apparently a Roman 1st-century piece, modelled on Classical Greek works. «**Diadumenes**» (E88) and «**Faun at rest**» (E 30) are Roman copies of famous Greek originals. The former, by Polyclitus, may be an athlete and an image of Apollo. The latter, by Praxiteles, is youthful and joyful image very typical of his style. A fully Roman work is very beautiful bust of

«**Antinous**»★ (E 60), a subject frequently chosen by the sculptors of Hadrian's Rome (this young Bithynian was a favourite of the Emperor); and also the delicate «**Venus with dolphin**» (E 31), the monumental «**Sleeping Ariadne**» (E 167) and the series of **Muses** which come from Hadrian's villa in Tivoli.

«Antinous»
arble 97 × 78 × 42 cm.
60)

Renaissance pieces include two lovely bronzes
bought by Velazquez in Italy: «**Espinarius**» (E
163) and «**Hermaphrodite**» (E 223), which was
the inspiration for Velazquez's «Rokeby Venus».
Other Renaissance works are the beautiful
bronzes of Charles V and members of his family,
by **Leon Leoni** and his son **Pompeo Leoni**. The
most outstanding of these is the powerful
«**Emperor Charles V and Fury**»★ (E 273), a
majestic, dignified group which has the added
curiosity that it can be dismantled: beneath the
Emperor's armour, his figure is carved as though
nude, and bears images recalling the ancient
Roman Emperors. Other bronze whole-body
statues, are models of «**The Empress Isabella**»★
(E 274), the Emperor's wife, and his son «**Philip
II**» (E 272). Dating from the same century are
two small sculptures, attributed to **El Greco**, of
«**Epimetheus and Pandora**» (E 483), once
considered to be figures of Adam and Eve.

The delightful 18th-century work «**Group of
Children**» (E 276) by the Italian **Agostino
Cornachini** is normally on exhibit. And, from
the 19th century, separated for a special reason
from other sculptures of this century on exhibit
in the Casón - because the Villanueva building
has preferred to keep it within its walls -is the
seated statue of «**Doña Isabel de Braganza**»
(E 1) by **Manuel Alvarez Cubero**, which has
been placed in the round the hall of the
Velázquez entrance.

Leon Leoni and Pompeo Le
«The Empress Isabel
Bronze 177 x 84 x 93
(E 2

Leon Leoni and Pompeo Le
«Emperor Charles V and Fu
Bronze 251 x 143 x 130
(E 2

The Decorative Arts

As well as Painting, Sculpture and an abundant collection of Drawings (generally not on exhibit), the Prado Museum possesses a rich heritage of items which come under the heading of the decorative arts - furniture, tapestries, coins and medals - of which unfortunately very few can be exhibited (again, for reasons of space); and even the small number of items which are on show pass almost unnoticed by visitors.

One part of the collection, however, which does have a special place in the Museum - it occupies two rooms - is the so-called **Dauphin's Treasure**. This is an exceptionally fine collection of precious wares which belonged to the Dauphin of France, Louis XIV's eldest son who died before he could accede to his father's throne. The line of accession passed to his eldest son, since the second, Philip of Anjou, had already been King of Spain since 1700. The Dauphin's treasure was Philip's part of the inheritance when the «jewels» which the Dauphin had collected were shared out. Philip V did not appreciate them very much - to the extent that he did not even order them to be taken out of their boxes.

Charles III valued the pieces more for the quality of their materials (agates, rock crystal...) than for any artistic beauty they might have, and arranged for them to go to the Natural History Museum. Along with other valuable goods, they were taken out of Spain by the French during the War of Independence; they were subsequently returned from France in 1815, with twelve pieces missing. In the middle of the 19th century, it was decided that they should be exhibited in the Prado Museum, since they were regarded as being of more artistic than material value. In 1918, eleven pieces were stolen, and several more were mutilated when the thieves removed the gold and precious stones. The current exhibition has special security arrangements.

Taking into consideration the materials, the pieces fall into two main groups: those made of semi-precious stones and those of rock crystal. The semi-precious stones include agates, jaspers, carnelians, lapis lazuli and turquoises. Agates, jaspers and carnelians are crystalline varieties of quartz: agates are very varied in colour, jaspers have more of a single overall colour, and carnelians are of only one colour, lighter and more translucent. The lapis lazuli seems to have come from Afghanistan and Russia. The turquoise is thought to have been brought from Persia or Egypt.

This group of pieces made from semi-precious stones is made up mainly of goblets, cups and trays, which are trimmed with gold and other precious metals, and also with enamels. They are also adorned with antique Roman, Mediaeval and Renaissance cameos which are portraits (there is one of Francis I and another of Cardinal Richelieu). They are also decorated with designs engraved on the stones showing scenes, human figures, monsters and mythological gods.

Rock crystal is a fine, beautiful material (colourless and transparent crystallised quartz) which was used from Roman times, throughout the Middle Ages; it became fashionable again in

e Renaissance, and workshops in Northern
aly were particularly renowned for it. The
rystal used in the Treasure is of excellent
uality, probably coming from the Swiss Alps.
his collection is mainly made up of goblets and
lasses of different shapes, although there are
lso serving dishes and trays. Most of the pieces
ere designed as drinking vessels, and these are
ecorated with designs relating to the theme of
rinking, such as wine harvesting, Bacchus,
Noah, Neptune...They are adorned with
rimmings of precious metals and various types
nd qualities of gemstones: there are red rubies,
erhaps from Burma and Ceylon, green emeralds
rom mines in the Tyrol, and diamonds (not of
ery high quality) probably from India.

he most emblematic piece in the collection, for
ts great originality, is the «**Onyx salt-cellar
with a gold mermaid**»★ (01); the receptacle is of
riental onyx, and the stem is a mermaid made
f gold with the lower part coated in enamel.
No doubt the mermaid is meant to evoke the
ea, the source of salt.

Along with the pieces themselves, some of their
pecially-made caskets are also displayed.

«**Onyx salt-cellar with a gold mermaid**»
17.5 cm. high
(01)

Francisco Pradilla. «Doña Juana the Madwoman» (detail)

19th Century Collection in the Casón del Buen Retiro

19th Century Collection in the Casón del Buen Retiro

The Prado Museum has a considerable number of 19th-century paintings —more than three thousand five hundred in total— of which only about ten per cent are exhibited. A small proportion of the rest is kept in the Casón's storerooms, with a larger number of works on loan to other institutions and museums. In addition, the nineteenth century collection includes some six hundred sculptures; those which are exhibited are chosen with the aim of providing artistic and historical background.

The Museum's 19th-century works were removed from the Prado in 1894 in order to create what was named the Modern and Contemporary Art Museum. They were returned to the Prado in 1971, together with many other 19th-century paintings which had been acquired over the years by the newer Museum, which was closing down that year. Its 20th-century paintings were used to make a Museum of Contemporary Art on the University Campus, whose stocks have since been transferred to the Reina Sofía National Contemporary Art Museum and Arts Centre.

The works which were returned to the Prado were assigned to a special 19th-century section, in a building which was given to the Museum for this purpose at the time: the Casón del Buen Retiro. The Casón (which means simply large house, a name it acquired in the late 19th century, apparently because of its bad state of repair) is thought to have been the Buen Retiro Palace Ballroom, and was built in the 17th century by the Count-Duke of Olivares for his sovereign Philip IV. Other remaining parts of the

Palace are the so-called Kingdoms Hall (Salón de Reinos) (currently the Army Museum) and its very large park (now smaller) which was named «the Retiro» (or the Retreat) after it.

The Casón still has the opulent ceiling decoration of the Grand Salon (on the ground floor) painted by Luca Giordano when the Casón was first built. The roof painting is dedicated to the noble order of Cavalrymen, the Toisón de Oro, which was headed by the King. In this large hall hang emblematic canvasses dealing with 19th-century historical subjects; around it are other rooms containing 20th-century paintings and sculpture.

The 19th-century paintings in the Casón del Buen Retiro are presented chronologically and according to style. This permits the visitor to follow a particular tour, which will be followed by this guide. The tour begins in the entrance hall on the ground floor (access via Alfonso XII street) and in the rooms to the right of this entrance, continues upstairs where it covers the whole floor, and ends in the remaining ground floor rooms (on the left).

The Casón's pieces belong to the five main successive (though overlapping) artistic movements of the 19th century: Neoclassicism, Romanticism, Realism, Impressionism and what has been termed «turn-of-the-century» painting. The exhibition starts off with Neoclassical painting, which developed in the early decades of the century. When we look at the early years of the 19th century, we inevitably notice that Goya is missing from this building; he lived until 1828 and his work anticipated many artistic

Vicente López
«The painter Francisco de Goya»
Canvas 935 × 770 cm.
(864)

trends of the 19th century (and even of the 20th). The only trace of him in the Casón is his magnificent portrait «**The painter Francisco de Goya**»★ (864) by **Vicente López** which occupies pride of place in the room where López's work is exhibited.

Before entering the painting rooms, the visitor will see three magnificent sculptures in the entrance hall. Although they were the property of the Prado Museum, for many years they graced the gardens of the National Library, being the site of the now defunct Modern Art Museum (see above). The sculpture entitled «**Sagunto**» (E889) is by **Agustín Querol**, and is a sculptural version of historical themes familiar to Romantic painting. The sculpture in the centre is the best example of Modernist sculpture which the Museum has to offer: it is by **Miguel Blay**, called «**Apparition**» (E 788), without doubt a late example of the aspects of late Romanticism which were taken up by Modernism. The group is completed by a much later, although still rather melodramatic, work; it is entitled «**Little milk brothers**» (E 890), by **Aniceto Marinas**, the Segovian sculptor who also made the statue of Velázquez which stands in the Main Entrance of the Villanueva building.

The rooms to the right of the entrance hall are given over to the Neo-Classical movement, inluding historical and allegorical paintings and portraits. Spanish **Neo-Classicism** has two main trends or facets: one which in reality is no more than Classical Academicism in the Baroque tradition (which in this country followed in the wake of Mengs' teachings) and another which is

a pure, French-style Neo-Classicism; both these movements developed alongside one another. Some figures painted in both modes, but the French Neo-Classicism of José Madrazo and Juan Antonio de Ribera developed earlier than that of Vicente López, who was without doubt the last great exponent of the ostentatious, eighteenth-century Baroque style, tinged with Classical Academicism.

José de Madrazo introduced European Neo-Classical ideals, which he became acquainted with at first hand in Paris as a follower of Louis David. The Neo-Classical system, based on a humble and devoted admiration of the Classical world, was obliged to seek its inspiration (given the lack of painting dating from remote Roman or Greek times) in sculpture, which had better withstood the ravages of time. Hence its most familiar characteristics: a lack of interest in colour and the predominance of line and painstaking academic drawing. «**The Death of Viriato**»★ (4469) by Madrazo is undoubtedly the most representative and most monumental picture in this style. Madrazo painted this canvas in Rome; when it became known in Spain, it had its great admirers, but also received some criticism.

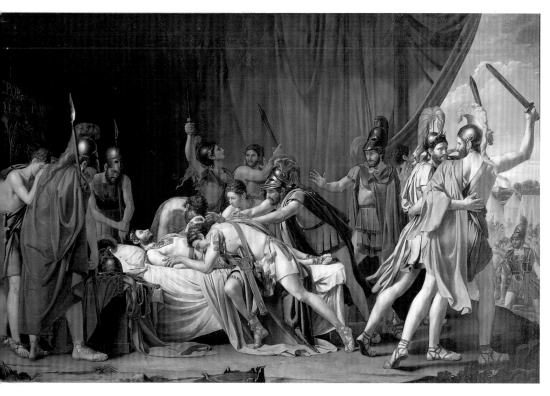

José de Madrazo
«The Death of Viriato»
Canvas 307 × 460 cm.
(4469)

There are two very fine (though less famous) pieces by the other great Neo-Classical painter, **Juan Antonio de Ribera**. These were painted as a pair —although at different times— and deal with two historical subjects: «**Cincinatus abandons the plough to make laws in Rome**» (5748) and «**Wamba renouncing the crown**» (6519); these paintings show Spanish Neo-Classicism at its best. Finally in this room, there are two elegant «**Allegories of the Seasons**» (5518 and 6492), also by Juan Antonio de Ribera, and an excellent landscape of the «view» genre: the «**View of the Retiro pond**» (4846) by **José Ribelles**.

The second room is also dedicated to Neo-Classicism, in this case the portrait in particular, although there are also some genre and historial paintings mixed in with these. Portraits which deserve special mention are that of the poet «**Manuel José Quintana**» (2904) by José Ribelles, the two group family portraits of the «**The Monarchs of Etruria**» (5221 and 5257), by different artists (**José Aparicio** and **Francisco Javier Fabré**) and, most importantly, the great portrait of «**Queen Isabella of Braganza**»★ (863), painted by **Bernardo López** at a later date. This was a posthumous portrait of the second wife of Ferdinand VII, glorifying her as the founder of the Prado Museum which first opened in the year after her death. This portrait was painted ten years after the inauguration, and must have been intended as a commemorative piece; the Queen is pictured pointing out of a window at the completed Museum building; with the other hand she is pointing out some plans for the distribution of the pictures in the rooms. Bernado López found his inspiration for the face of the deceased Queen in a portrait of her painted by his father, the Court painter Vicente López, which is hanging in the next room. We can also see works by two anonymous Neo-Classical painters (one French, the other Italian), on two attractive mythological themes: «**Venus curing Aeneas**» (6075) and «**Ulysses commending Telemachus to the care of others**» (4713). There are also portraits by **Rafael Tejeo** and a «**Self-portrait**» (4470) by José de Madrazo.

ernardo López
«Queen Maria Isabella of Braganza»
anvas 254 × 172 cm.
863)

Vicente López Portaña, the main artist in the next room, succeeded Goya as painter to the King, but did not follow in his footsteps stylistically. On the contrary, he is regarded as having taken a step backwards —reversing the advances achieved by Goya. He was a painter of extraordinary talents, which he used to make an important contribution to the new Neo-Classicism, as well as being the last great exponent of eighteenth-century Baroque. The lace, ringlets and brooches with which he drapes his sitters and which he takes such pleasure in depicting, are reminiscent of «rococo», then in decline.

The room devoted to López seems to be dominated by his magnificent portrait of Goya (see above). He took over from the Master as Court painter to Ferdinand VII, whose portrait he painted many times. At an earlier period, while working as a painter in Valencia, he painted the group portrait of the family of the previous monarch, Charles IV: it is entitled **«Painting to commemorate the visit of Charles IV to the University of Valencia»** (2815), executed two years after Goya's portrait of the same family. In this case, the portrait is allegorical, and figures symbolising the University of Valencia accompany the royal sitters: the different Faculties, Peace, Victory and the goddess Minerva. The portrait of **«Ferdinand VII»** (7114) on exhibit was the first one López painted of the new king, and it became the model for all the subsequent ones. His portraits of the king's four wives are also on exhibit: **«María Antonia of Bourbon, Princess of Asturias»** (868), **«María Isabella of**

Braganza» (809), **«María Josefa Amalia of Saxony»** (867) and **«María Cristina of Bourbon»**⋆ (865); he was also drawing instructor to the three latter. A sculpture by **Jos Piquer** is also in the room; Piquer was Royal Sculptor at the same time that López was painter; it depicts **«Saint Jerome penitent»** (E 719), which Queen Isabella II commissioned to be cast in bronze.

The next room contains two sculptures by the Venetian sculptor **Antonio Canova**, one by the Danish artist **Bertel Thorwaldsen** and four **«Allegories»** (4471, 4472, 5822, 5823) by **José de Madrazo**, representing the four times of day Dawn, Midday, Dusk and Night.

Vicente López Portaña
«María Cristina of Bourbon»
Canvas 96 × 75 cm.
(365)

In the passage leading to the stairway which in turn leads to the upper floor, a large, later work by **German Pérez Amores** is on exhibit. It shows «**Socrates scolding Alcibiades in a courtesan's house**» (6806), a very carefully executed composition in a Classical setting. The subject is taken from Plato's Dialogues, and refers to Alcibiades' renouncing the strict doctrines of his Master Socrates which teach the impropriety of the pleasures of the flesh. Right at the foot of the stairs is the delightful sculpture «**Faith, Hope and Charity**» (E 787) by **Felipe Moratilla**. Another, somewhat later historical painting of great beauty and transcendence is on display in the stairwell: «**The Surrender of Bailén**» (4265) by **José Casado del Alisal**, better viewed from the top of the staircase. This depicts the first great defeat of the French, in the War of Independence. The surrender of Marshall Dupont's troops to General Castaño depicted by Casado del Alisal is clearly a homage to Velázquez's «The Lances», recalling the earlier work in the composition of its groups, and evoking the same skilful, realistic interpretation of the theme.

The exhibition continues on the upper floor with four successive rooms given over to **Romanticism**. The Romantic period of painting was a rich epoch in Spanish art history, despite having turned its back on the Romantic (and not only pre-Romantic) innovations of Goya. Again, foreign influences produced a change of direction, and ironically, it was through foreign influences that Spain was able to re-establish the great cultural tradition which had flourished in its own Golden Age.

Spanish Romanticism manifests two main trends, though these are not always clearly distinguishable from one another. The exhibition begins with the so-called colourist or sketchist «bravura» movement; the painters who represent this style took up both methods and subjects which had been discarded since Goya. Their method is based on free, irregular, apparently spontaneous brushwork. The first room offers an excellent selection of the work of one of these painters, **Eugenio Lucas**, who copied Goya's technique to the extent that sometimes his paintings have been confused with those of the great Aragonese Master. The themes are often the same as Goya's: thus in this room we can see a very Goyaesque work «**Bullfighting with pikes**» (4421), a work which inevitably recalls Goya's Majas «**The Presidents' Wives**» (4426), and even three about the Inquisition, among which we would point out specially the one entitled «**Condemned by the Inquisition**» (6974). The room is dominated by «**The Hunter**» (4424), which is clearly reminiscent of Velázquez.

Eugenio Lucas
«The Presidents' Wives»
Canvas 72 × 55 cm.
(4426)

Within the same movement, **Leonardo Alenza** chose popular customs as his subjects. Several works of his are on exhibit in the next room on the left/right. Two small ones are particularly interesting: the tiny «**The beating**»★ (4207), inspired by an engraving by Goya entitled «... if the jug gets broken» , and the also very small «**Galician puppeteer**» (4205), also called «Punch and Judy». Also in the room are some excellent Romantic landscapes. On the subject of landscape and its importance in Spanish 19th-century painting, it should be remembered that up till then, Spanish art had not looked seriously at landscape. This did not stop El Greco, Velázquez and Goya producing some of the best landscapes ever painted, but landscape as a subject of a painting in itself belongs to the 19th century. In Romanticism, the key figures were encouraged to devote their time to landscape when they saw the interest foreign landscape artists seemed to take in the Spanish landscape (in Europe as a whole, landscape had been established as a subject from the Baroque period onwards) such as the British artist **David Roberts** (some of whose works are exhibited in the Prado). The most important figure is **Jenaro Pérez Villaamil**, whose «**Herd of Bulls by a River**» (6994) and «**View of the Castle of Gaucin**» (6754) are on show. In the latter, the artist is shown painting his own portrait beside one of the contemplative highwaymen. There is also a work by **Francisco Lemeyer**, who has been called the «Spanish Delacroix», entitled «**Moors in Combat**» (4395).

In the next two rooms we can see the other main movement within Romanticism beginning to dominate. This is represented by painters who, due to their Neo-Classical training, always remained deeply attached to drawing and line; this artistic education aligned them more with the ideas of European Romanticism. Above all, in these two rooms we can see the works of **Antonio María Esquivel**, including two important paintings, one in each room. The one entitled «**The Fall of Lucifer**» (7569) is one of his best works, inasmuch as he painted it to donate to the Lyceum of Art and Literature, an institution which helped him greatly during his temporary blindness: its careful execution is no doubt partly due to the fact that it was going to be examined and evaluated by many of his colleagues in that institution. The other canvas, in the other room, is the well-known «**Contemporary Poets**»★ (4299) also entitled «Poets' Meeting»; this magnificent group portrait shows José Zorilla in the centre, reading some of his poems aloud in front of an audience of fellow members of his circle, gathered in the studio of the painter himself, who also appears in the centre in front of his canvas.

Leonardo Alenza
«The beating»
Canvas 330 × 245 cm.
(4207)

tonio María Esquivel
ontemporary Poets»
nvas 144 × 217 cm.
299)

The most important artists of the next rooms are undoubtedly Federico de Madrazo (especially his portraits), the great pillar of Spanish Romanticism, and one of the best Spanish portraitists of all time, and Carlos Luis de Ribera. In the 19th century, the portrait was extremely widespread in comparison with previous centuries, when few portraits were painted, and the sitters were drawn from a narrow social range. While in the 16th and 17th centuries, portraiture was limited to the monarchy and aristocracy, from the 18th century onwards, and especially in this part of the 19th, portraiture was be the domain of the bourgeosie proper and of the ever more numerous middle classes who wanted to imitate and join it. **Carlos Luis de Ribera** was the son (as was Federico de Madrazo) of another great Neo-Classical artist and so was a lover of line and drawing. Among his portraits, the charming «**Portrait of a child**» (4597), in the first room, is particularly outstanding. Nevertheless, its particular charm contrasts sharply with the consciosly tragic presentation of the large canvas which dominates the room: «**The daughters of El Cid**» (4588), carefully executed by **Diáscoro Téofilo de La Puebla**. A portrait by **Federico de Madrazo**, offering an introduction to the next room, is also on display: that of the singer «**Sofía Vela**» (4449) with its magnificent effect of light falling on the musical score and on the hand holding it.

The next space is occupied entirely by works by Federico de Madrazo. Note particulary the portrait of «**the Countess of Vilches**»* (2878) which is remarkable for being one of the most cheerfully colourful of his works, and also that of the young «**Federico Flores**» (4452), being one of the few which show a landscape in the background.

The next room is dominated by the large historical canvas by **Eduardo Cano**, entitled «**The Burial of Alvaro de Luna**» (4262), whose subject is explained in the long title under which the canvas was entered for the 1868 National Exhibition. To summarize: «Don Alvaro de Luna, constable and favourite of King John II of Castile, publicly beheaded in Valladolid Main Square, on 2nd June 1453, is given a charitable burial in the cemetery for executed prisoners outside the city walls». Other portraits by Madrazo are also on display in this room, such as the exquisite portrait of the Romantic writer «**Carolina Coronado**» (4451).

derico de Madrazo
he Countess of Vilches»
nvas 123 × 87 cm.
78)

In the narrow room which follows, the visitor can see works depicting popular customs and themes, another characteristic aspect of Romanticism, along with to the popular notion of Spain as an exotic, almost «oriental» country which was current at the time. Spain, its customs, and its traditions, became fashionable. Some Spanish artists highlighted the existence of this Spanish world of popular folklore, which found a good market both abroad and amongst the country's own bourgeoisie. The authorities also promoted this type of ethnologically documented, popular painting from the different regions of Spain. Two fine folklore paintings of this type are on exhibit: «**The procession of the Corpus Christi in Seville**» (4259) by **Manuel Cabral** and «**The courtyard of the stables in the former bullring in Madrid, before a bullfight**» (4272) by **Manuel Castellano**. In the next room we can see paintings by Valeriano Domínguez Bécquer and Manuel Rodrigo de Guzmán. **Valeriano Domínguez Bécquer** (brother of the poet) received a pension (today it would be called a grant) from what was then called the Ministry of Cultural Development, to study and paint the different types of Spanish people, costumes and customs. The pictures «**The Present**» (4237) and «**The Dance**» (4234), showing folklore scenes from Aragón and Soria, are from this series (which he did not complete). Of the work of **Manuel Rodríguez de Guzmán**, a follower of Bécquer, and like him one of a long line of painters from the same Sevillian family, note especially «**Santiponce Fair**» (4604).

There are also a few landscape works in this room, such as «**Exterior view of Burgos Cathedral**». On the other hand, the next room given over almost entirely to landscapes, here in a realist style; this group of works is based on a collection of the work of **Carlos de Haes**, which the Museum possesses thanks to the bequest made by the painter to his followers, and the donation they in turn made to what was then the Modern Art Museum. Although Carlos de Haes painted his compositions in his studio, he based them on sketches taken directly from Nature; hence he is an early exponent of Realism (whereas the Romantics in fact invented imaginary landscapes). Among his works, which are mostly on a small scale, «**Los Picos de Europa**»★ (4390) is particularly notable. It depicts a high mountain pass, skilfully recreated by Haes using greens and blues. Other landscape artists are represented in this room: **Juan Espín** with his «**Granadan Landscape**» (4677), **Ramón Martí Alsina** with «**Landscape with a flock**» (7053) and **Antonio Muñoz Degrain**, working somewhat later, with «**Landscape on Pardo Mount**» (4518).

In the elongated room which follows, really a passageway, is a small exhibition of the Museum's foreign painting collection. Note particularly the amiable, sensual and hedonist style of the French painter **Paul Baudry** in «**The pearl and the wave**» (2604), a beautiful female nude which, though painted in the mid-19th century, recalls the rococo style. The Dutch painter **Lawrence Alma Tadema**, who later became a British national and was honoured with a knighthood, painted «**Pompeyan Scene**» (3996) which is full of reminiscences of ancient Rome.

arlos de Haes
«Los Picos de Europa»
anvas 168 × 123 cm.
1390)

The next room is one of the most pleasing in the Cason, since it contains beautiful pieces by the internationally renowned and successful painters Fortuny and Raimundo de Madrazo; it also has pieces by Martín Rico.

Mariano Fortuny had a high reputation throughout Europe, equalled only by that enjoyed by Picasso in the 20th century. He and his contemporary Eduardo Rosales are the two most important figures of the century, comparable only with Goya (who lived nearly thirty years into the same century). Fortuny's style is dextrous and confident, with flowing technique. His works include the tiny «**Nude on Portici beach**» (2606) painted while was in Italy, and the equally small scale group portrait of **Moroccans**» (2607) which are a reminder of his travels in North Africa; this trip was funded by Barcelona City Council to record the exploits of Catalan soldiers in the Moroccan war. He also painted the extremely direct «**Old man naked in the sun**» (2612) and, lastly but importantly, «**The artist's children in the Japanese Hall**»★ (2931). In this picture, which was definitely not a commissioned piece, Fortuny experimented with various painting techniques: the little girl's legs are perfectly outlined, rounded and seem almost real, while in other parts of the painting, the brushstrokes are so free, loose and distinct from one another that they anticipate Impressionism. The paintings entitled «**Corral**» (4357) and «**Bullfight**» (4328) also anticipate this movement.

Very beautiful portraits by **Raimundo de Madrazo** are on exhibit here: for example, the

two portraits of «**The Model Aline Masson**» (2621 and 2622), and the one of «**Queen Maria Christina**» (2619) who was governor and the mother of Alfonso XIII. **Martín Rico**'s landscapes further enhance an already valuable collection this room, especially the highly decorative «**View of Paris**» (7173).

There are more works by Raimundo de Madrazo in the next room and also many beautiful paintings by Vicente Palmaroli; the Rosales exhibits also start here. **Eduardo Rosales** was the social and personal opposite of the successful Fortuny: the only thing they had in common was that both died young. Rosales' style reflects his character: often serious, solemn and austere, especially in comparison with Fortuny's charm and brilliance. In this room, a small picture of his is exhibited, entitled «**The Presentation of John of Austria to Charles V**» (4610), which reveals his gifts as a colourist more than his other works, as does the portrait of the teenage daughter of General Serrano, the «**Countess of Santovenia**» (6711), a symphony in shades of pink.

Also by Rosales, in the following room, a magnificent historical work is on display (a genre which has continued to be important since Romanticism) «**The Deatch of Lucretia**» (4613) Near this we can see a preliminary sketch of his more famous historical work «**The Last Will and Testament of Isabella the Catholic Monarch**» (4618) which is exhibited in the Grand Salon. «The Death of Lucretia» is on an ancient Classical subject: the suicide of this Roman patrician after being raped by the

Mariano Fortuny
«The artist's children in the Japanese Hall»
Canvas 44 × 93 cm.
(2931)

son of King Tarquin the Proud. Beside it is
another historical work, by **Lorenzo Valles**,
entitled «**Joan the Madwoman**» (4669). This
character was a frequent subject of 19th-century
historical painting. Opposite these works hangs
the enormous painting «**Queen María Cristina
inspecting the troops**» (4332) by Fortuny.

The two main artists exhibited in the next room are **Ignacio Pinazo** and **Francisco Domingo Marqués**, whose works are also displayed in the following room. The work of both of these Valencian artists sometimes offer glimpses of the technique of the **Impressionists**; free brushwork and a creative interest in light, which Sorolla, also a Valencian, was to devote himself to. Sorolla is a clear example of that particular facet of Spanish Impressionism, called «luminism». The two former artists preseved an interest in realism and a certain tendency to use dark colours. Of Pinazo's work, note especially **«Learning by Heart»** (4576), the light, soft **«Self- portrait»** (4582) and the lovely child portrait of **«Ignacio, the artist's son»** (4574). Among Domingo Marqués' work, his **«Self-portrait»** (4489) is also particularly worthy of mention, as is the freely rendered **«Portal of the Marquis of Dos Aguas in Valencia»** (4486).

There are works by **Joaquín Sorolla** in the next two rooms. In the first, **«They say fish is still expensive»** (4649), is worthy of note, a late example of «social» realism in painting, which did not manifest itself in Spain at the same time as in other countries, because Spain lagged behind in the Industrial Revolution. The portrait of **«María Guerrero»** (4647) is also on exhibit; this depicts a famous actress, dressed for the part of Lady Foolish from the play by Lope de Vega; behind her we can see her husband, also a famous actor, Fernando Díaz de Mendoza. The second room is lit up by the splendid work **«Children at the beach»**★ (4648), donated to the now defunct Modern Art Museum by Sorolla himself, a few years before his death. It is worthwhile taking a closer look at the

magnificent skill displayed in the light touches of colour with which Sorolla manages to convey the bright reflection of the sun on the wet bodies of the children sprawled in the sand.

In the same room is a historical work intended a a splendid painting for a study or library, **«Francisco Pradilla's** work entitled **«Queen Joan the «Madwoman», on retreat in Tordesillas with her daughter the infanta Catalina»** (7493). The deranged queen was one of Pradilla's favourite themes throughout his career; he painted her on many occasions after having great success with the first canvas he painted depicting one moment in her tormented life —painted thirty years before this one— which is on exhibit in the Grand Salon of the Museum. In this one, Joan appears to be unaware, in her demented state, of the affectionate approach of her younger daughter, on retreat with her at Tordesillas; undoubtedly the little girl and her toys give the scene its lively tone.

The next room opens with another work by Pradilla —the exquisite «Large-scale miniature», as it has been called —which depicts the **«Baptismal Cortège of prince Juan, son of the Catholic Monarchs, proceeding through the streets of Seville»** (7601). This was painted four years later than the previous painting, and is undoubtedly the masterpiece of Pradilla's maturer years; although its theme puts it in the category of «historical painting», its mode of presentation makes it more like a kind of bourgeois chronicle. Each and every one of the figures which make up this complex scene are worked with the same loving attention to detail.

Joaquín Sorolla
«Children at the beach»
Canvas 118 × 185 cm.
(4648)

The other artist exhibited in this room is **Aureliano de Beruete**, a painter whose work, like Sorolla's, developed at the beginning of the 20th century. Beruete was an exceptional landscape artist, creating a colourful and luminous version of Impressionism. A good part of the landscapes on display here depict various views of Madrid; note especially «**The Manzanares River**» (4252), «**The Banks of the Manzanares**» (4248) and «**The Guadarrama**»★ (4254). «**Winter landscape. Princes' Garden**» (4057) uses a rich range of greens, pinks, purples, yellows and other warm, subtle tones, making it one of his liveliest works.

The Exhibition continues on the ground floor, as indicated at the beginning of this section of the guide, in the rooms to the left at the the bottom of the stairs. The first of these rooms contains (like the last room on the upper floor) turn-of-the-century painting, here concentrating on basically Catalan painters, including interesting works by Francisco Gimeno, Santiago Rusiñol, Isidro Nonell and Joaquín Mir. There are two attractive landscapes by **Francisco Gimeno**, a landscape artist whose work anticipated developments in modern expressionism, entitled «**Secluded Spot**» (4345) and «**Aigua Blava**» (4346). **Santiago Rusiñol**'s landscape work (he was the most significant exponent of Modernism through landscape) is represented here by his «**Garden in Aranjuez**»★ (4630); his portraiture is demonstrated by the portrait of «**Sarah Bernhardt**» (7019). **Isidro Nonell**, whose aesthetic ideas were always original, is represented by only one work, called «**Flat roof**». Two works are exhibited by **Joaquín Mir**,

the great innovator in landscape; note especially «**The Orchard and the Hermitage**» (4514). There are also works by non-Catalan artists, such as the original **Agustín Riancho** and the unusual and complex **Darío de Regoyos**. The former's beautiful work «**Tree**» (4593) is exhibited, along with four paintings by the latter, of which one of the two depicting «**The beach in San Sebastián**» (4590) and especially the delicate, freely worked «The Vineyard» are particularly worth seeing. **José María López Mezquita**'s work «**Line of Prisoners**» stands out, its severity contrasting with the landscapes in the room as does the palid tragedy of «**The Garrotting**» by Ramón Casas. «**Houses in Segovia**» painting by **Ignacio Zuloaga** serves as a point of connection between this room and the next.

Aureliano de Beruete
«The Guadarrama»
Canvas 56 × 102,5 cm.
(4254)

Santiago Rusiñol
«Garden in Aranjuez»
Canvas 134,5 × 140,5 cm.
(4630)

Among the works by Zuloaga which are exhibited in the next room, the visitor can see a genre painting called «**Young village bullfighters**», a stark religious work «**Christ of Blood**», and a pleasant portrait of «**Mrs. Alice Lolita Muth Maacha**»★ (2983). Ignacio Zuloaga was the painter who carried the spirit and aesthetic of the Spanish painting tradition through into the 20th century; it almost seems as if he draws his expressive force from El Greco, and his dramatic sense of colour from Velázquez and Goya. Zuloaga's works share the room with those by other painters. Particularly noteworthy are «**Bersolaris**» and «**Village authorities**» by **Valentín** and **Ramón Zubiaurre** respectively, and **Eduardo Chicharro**'s representation of «**Pain**».

Either of the two doors which open onto this one lead to the Grand Salon where the most famous «historical» paintings in the Museum's collection are on display. Leaving the next room, where the Museum's final exit is to be found, we enter the Grand Salon.

This Granad Salon is the room which best represents the Casón del Buen Retiro. The ceiling which arches above it is decorated with a painting by **Luca Giordano**, as a decorative homage to the Spanish monarchy. Its subject is «**Allegory of the Toisón del Oro**», which was the medal of honour created by the Dukes of Burgundy and brought to Spain by Charles I, from then on passing into the hands of the House of Austria. The allegory was painted during the reign of this dynasty's last monarch, Charles II.

The large canvasses exhibited beneath this Baroque ceiling are some of the most representative and famous examples of Historical Painting anywhere; the seven on show were painted between 1864 and 1899.

The earliest work here is «**The Last Will and Testament of Isabella the Catholic Monarch**»★ (4625) by **Eduardo Rosales**. This canvas was awarded prizes in the 1864 Exhibition, and also in Paris in 1867, where it earned Rosales a gold medal and also the decoration of the Legion of Honour, awarded by Napoleon III. It depicts the Queen on her deathbed dictating her will to a scribe, in the presence of her downcast husband King Fernando, accompanied by her daughter and heir, princess Joan —on the left of the compsition— and two groups of people on either side of the foot of the bed; among those in the foreground, note the figure of Cardinal Cisneros, who was to act as Regent of Castilla after the Queen's death.

Eduardo Rosales
«The Last Will and Testament of Isabella the Catholic Monarch»
Canvas 290 x 400 cm
(4625)

Ignacio Zuloaga
«Mrs. Alice Lolita Muth Maacha»
Canvas 75 × 56 cm.
(2983)

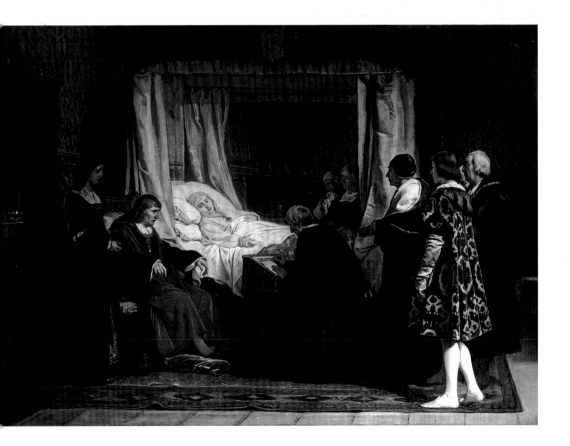

The work «**Doña Juana the Madwoman**»★ (4584) by **Francisco Pradilla** is on display; it is his definitive masterpiece, and brought him immediate international recognition. It depicts Joan the Madwoman stopping on the long journey she made to take the corpse of her husband, Philip the Handsome, to Granada. The demented princess made the funeral cortège travel only at night, while by day the coffin was taken to some church or monastery. On this occasion, she ordered it to be removed and taken into the countryside, having realised that the place where the coffin had been taken was a convent of nuns, and not a monastery.

José Moreno Carbonero created «**Prince Charles of Viana**» (6802) which paints a picture of the unfortunate and fiction-like life of this prince, who was halfbrother of Ferdinand the Catholic King; their father, John II of Aragon, preferred the latter as successor, and Charles withdrew to a secluded life of reading, which is evoked by the painting.

«**The lovers of Teruel**» (4511) by **Antonio Muñoz Degrain** was based on the legendary tale of the unfortunate lovers Isabel de Segura and Diego Martínez de Mansanilla, whose love story has a tragic ending. The picture is exceptionally fine in both the brightly lit foreground, and in the background, where the figures can barely be made out in the semi-darkness.

José Moreno Carbonero painted his «**Conversion of the Duke of Gandía**» (6565) in the same year as «The lovers» was made, 1884, when he was only twenty-four. Both pictures were entered and awarded prizes at that year's Exhibition. This painting is about Francisco de Borja (fourth Duke of Gandía), who renounced worldy things when he saw the rotting corpse o what had been the extremely beautiful Empress Isabella, wife of Charles V. Gandía's feelings are summed up in the later famous phrase «Never again shall I serve a mortal lord». Francisco de Borja abandoned the world, entered the Company of Jesus, and became a saint.

«**The execution of Torrijos and his comrades on the beaches at Malaga**»★ (4368) by **Antonio Gisbert** was painted four years later. It was not painted with the intention of competing in any Exhibition, but was an official commission made by Sagasta's Liberal Government during María Cristina's period of rule (when Isabella II was too young to act as monarch). The purpose of the commission, which was done by Royal Decree, was to recreate the execution of the participants in the uprising, which gave rise to the Liberal Triennial of Ferdinand VII, when he recovered his absolute power; the work was intended to represent the defence of liberties.

Antonio Gisbe
«The Execution of Torrijos and his comrade
on the beaches at Malaga
Canvas 390 × 600 cn
(4368

Francisco Pradilla
«Doña Juana the Madwoman»
Canvas 340 × 500 cm.
(4584)

«The Expulsion of the Jews from Spain»
(6578) was painted by **Emilio Sala** while he was living on an artist's pension in Paris. He exhibited it in the Universal Exhibition which took place there in 1888. This historical theme was not fashionable at the time, and the subject was poorly understood by the public. In the canvas, the Catholic Monarchs are seen beneath a canopy on which their popular name can be made out; in front of them, we see the Inquisitor Torquemada violently interrupting the audience which the monarchs had granted to the Jews' negotiator.

ndex relates the catalogue numbers that appear on the descriptive card or frame of each one of the exhibited works with
mber of the page on which it is cited in this guide. The bold numbers refer to the illustrations. The catalogue numbers
ed by the letter "S" indicate works of sculpture.

This index relates the catalogue numbers that appear on the descriptive card or frame of each one of the exhibited works with the number of the page on which it is cited in this guide. The bold numbers refer to the illustrations. The catalogue numbers preceded by the letter "S" indicate works of sculpture.

© ALDEASA ®: 1994
Copyright deposit: M-5696-1999
ISBN: 84-8003-131-X

Cover: Velázquez **"Las Meninas"** (detail)

General co-ordination: Aldeasa
Design: Mar Lissón, Natalia Arranz
Photography: Museo del Prado Oronoz
Photo-composition: Grafitex, S.A., Barcelona
Photo-mechanics: Gamacolor, Madrid
Printed by: E. G. E., S.A.

(Printed in Spain)